church growth
from an
african american
perspective

DONALD HILLIARD JR.

FOREWORD BY HENRY H. MITCHELL

JUDSON PRESS
PUBLISHERS SINCE 1824
VALLEY FORGE

CHURCH GROWTH FROM AN AFRICAN AMERICAN PERSPECTIVE

Library of Congress Cataloging-in-Publication Data
Hilliard, Donald.
Church growth from an African American perspective / Donald Hilliard, Jr.
p. cm.
ISBN 0-8170-1495-0 (alk. paper)
1. African American churches. 2. Church growth—United States. I. Title.
BR563.N4H55 2006
254'.508996073—dc22
                                                                    2006002845
Printed in the U.S.A.

14 13 12 11 10 09 08 07 06   10 9 8 7 6 5 4 3 2 1

To the greater glory of God,

in gratitude to the Cathedral International family,

in honor of Deacon Carlton Lane,

in celebration of the ministry of the

Rev. Dr. B. Glover-Williams,

and, finally, to the blessed memory of

Elder Robert Chapman and Charles Jonathon Barnes

contents

⊠ ⊠ ⊠ ⊠ ⊠ ⊠

Foreword	vi
Acknowledgments	vii
Preface	x

PART ONE

⊠

fundamentals for a growing church

1. Understanding Church Growth	2
2. Preparing for Growth	13
3. Foundations for Healthy Church Growth	23
4. Principles of Healthy Church Growth	40

PART TWO

⊠

practical dimensions

5. Purposeful Prayer	54
6. Prophetic Preaching	66
7. Powerful Worship	79
8. Pertinent Ministry	93
9. Practical Christian Education	110
10. Growing a Church through Multiplication	121
11. The Church at Its Best	136
Notes	148

foreword

⊠ ⊠ ⊠ ⊠ ⊠ ⊠

The subject of church growth has drawn the written attention of many people working out of a vast variety of experiences. Although Dr. Donald Hilliard's offering here comes out of his labor in the African American church, his wise, clear, and simple guidance through the complexities of change and growth in modern-day congregations can apply to any cultural or ethnic group. The folkways of worship and church organization vary more today by socioeconomic types than by ethnic groups, except where languages other than English are involved.

This breadth of application is due in part to the fact that this book, while part "how-to," is largely a spiritual and attitudinal guide. The growth churches seek is to be found more in a proper spiritual condition than in a particular combination of structural strategies and communication techniques. The fact that Hilliard has succeeded and is succeeding in church growth would suggest that his working balance between spirit and method is based on the same proportions of which he writes.

The details of organization provided herein are appropriately less emphasized but not overlooked. The spiritual maturity to which greater attention is given is likely to yield considerable success for any sensible system. In fact, sensible systems are sought and employed precisely because of the inevitable thoughtfulness that goes with spiritual maturity. In this same sensible vein is the low-key stance of the author, making no exaggerated claims for the effectiveness of his ministry. No book can work miracles in the complex world of volunteer churchmanship, but the approach of this book, if carefully and patiently followed, offers considerable promise.

—Henry H. Mitchell, Th.D.

church growth from an african american perspective

acknowledgments

⊠ ⊠ ⊠ ⊠ ⊠ ⊠

Deeming it impossible to thank all of the persons whose lives and experiences have intersected to make our ministry fruitful and this book possible, let me use this means to express my most profound appreciation to many of them.

I am appreciative of Linda Peavy and Randy Frame for their generous invitation to become a part of the distinguished Judson Press team of authors. I am especially thankful for their patience. The staff at Judson Press is rendering a tremendous service to the body of Christ, and I have benefited richly from their mass of resources throughout the years of my pastorate.

I would also like to thank my editorial and research assistant, Minister Christopher Michael Jones, for making it possible for me to get this manuscript completed in a timely fashion, as well as for serving formally as a most able pastoral liaison to the Cathedral International. Special thanks are to be extended to my executive assistant minister, Paula Simone Hankerson, and to her assistant, Giavonni Wallace, for always making me look better than I deserve and for handling many multifaceted responsibilities.

I appreciate the time and effort extended by my chief operating officer, Rhonda Anderson, in reading the manuscript and picking up little things that I may have missed. I am grateful for Dr. Henry Mitchell, whose timeless insight and pastoral reflections have influenced my ministry in many ways. I am equally grateful for Timothy Holmes, audio/video coordinator of Cathedral Productions, for pulling together the necessary materials from the Cathedral archives to help the writing process along.

I offer special thanks to my beloved wife of twenty-five years, Minister Phyllis Thompson-Hilliard, an author, preacher, and teacher, for her support. I am grateful also for our precious children—Leah, Charisma, and Destiny—who have supported all of my endeavors, and for my dear mother, Alease Hilliard-Chapman, for remaining, after all these years, one of my greatest cheerleaders. My family provides balance for me and gives me a place to come in from the cold.

I give thanks also for the saints of Cathedral International— One Church in Three Locations—Perth Amboy, Asbury Park, and Plainfield, New Jersey. These wonderful people, and many who are now in heaven, have tolerated my pastoral leadership for twenty-two years and have been a tremendous blessing to me. I give special thanks to the life and legacy of Deacon Carlton Lane and to the sacred memory of Elder Robert Chapman, Mattian Moore-McCoy, Joyce Coakley-Gilmore, Minister Hope McLean-Alston, Mother Leona Allen, Mother Gledora Soanes, Mother Olive Godfrey, and the countless other souls who have influenced my life. I thank the Lord for my having been blessed by their loving-kindness.

I was called to the Perth Amboy community in October of 1983 to serve as the seventy-second pastor of Second Baptist Church, and was installed in November of that year. It continues to be a wonderful, exciting, faith-filled and Spirit-led journey. I never would have dreamed that the small brick church building on Broad Street with a membership of 125 would have yielded the fruit of more than twelve properties. We have operated a restaurant and have started a daycare, a fully accredited school, and a counseling center. We have operated a florist shop, built townhouses, renovated a theater, and purchased a life center, two buildings, and one of the largest properties in Perth Amboy, all to the glory of God.

I firmly believe that a church should change the city, and this is what we are doing. At this writing (early in 2006) we anticipate breaking ground on 100 acres of land. But we also continue to grow where we are, having recently dedicated the new Jennifer's Joy in the City Child Development Center, the

church growth from an african american perspective

Cathedral Community Counseling Center, and the Cathedral Community Bible Institute, moving them all into the Cathedral Community Affairs complex, the hub of the daily administration of the church. And we have totally refurbished the Mercy House, which provides food, clothing, and emergency shelter for those in need.

I feel most undeserving of all the success that has come our way, but I give the Lord the glory and the people—the kind membership of the Cathedral, the Second Baptist Church—my heartfelt thanks.

preface

🞝 🞝 🞝 🞝 🞝 🞝

So those who welcomed his message were baptized, and that
day about three thousand persons were added.
—Acts 2:41, NRSV

Many reasons have been given for how and why a church should
grow. Typically, powerful preaching, teaching, worship, evangelism, discipleship, witnessing, fellowship, and service all are
attributed to the embodiment of the gospel. Along with these
normative practices, some include complex multimedia marketing, national conferences, community development, state and
federal funding, corporate partnership, health and financial services, school chartering, demographic research, publishing, aes-
thetics, and more as being among the major or minor contribu-
tors to church growth.

While scholars agree that the study of congregations is like a
dance between ecclesiology and the social-cultural reality in
which each church is fixed, many find difficulty in locating the
accounts, artifacts, and activities that undergird the church-
growth phenomenon. In other words, if we, the church, merely
administrate treasures deposited in earthen vessels, to what
extent should we claim credit for what God has done when the
church grows, especially if the gospel is always deposited in clay?

Certainly in the African American context, the gospel is the central focus and the "generator" of the church. When it is preached
with a high sense of commitment and integrity, the church grows,
not just numerically, but spiritually. Moreover, growing churches—who hear the gospel preached with integrity—have a godly
sense of vision and purpose; they reach, sow, and send. They tell
you why they do what they do, and not just how.

Growing churches typically have a particular leadership style, one that reflects authority. Good leaders focus on reaching people in obedience to the Lord Jesus Christ, and not merely on developing temporal institutions. In growing churches, preachers recognize that they do not have all of the spiritual gifts the Bible proclaims. So they delegate—share the responsibility of growing the vineyard in which they have been planted.

Most important, growing churches recognize that Jesus Christ is the author and finisher of the work. Any approach to understanding church growth must start with the will of God. Vision, the centrality of Christ, biblical preaching, purposeful prayer, dynamic worship, sound doctrine, comprehensive Christian education, holy living, tithing, and an orientation toward loving people all undergird the intentions of the pastor who desires to participate in the growth of the Lord's church. However, it is the Lord Jesus Christ who authenticates the pastor's intent.

The author of these chapters, Bishop Donald Hilliard Jr., has served as pastor to the Cathedral International—the historic Second Baptist Church of Perth Amboy, New Jersey—for more than twenty-two years. A man of integrity, Bishop Hilliard's tenure at the Cathedral International has been marked by triumph and tragedy, praise and perseverance, holy hands and handcuffs, anointing and adversity. In the midst of life's trials and tribulations, Bishop Hilliard has managed to unapologetically "say yes" to the Lord Jesus Christ.

Bishop Hilliard has served as adjunct professor at various theological seminaries, including The School of Theology, Boston University; Princeton Theological Seminary; and New Brunswick Theological Seminary. He has also served as group convener and mentor to the Donald Hilliard Fellows Doctor of Ministry Program at The School of Theology, Drew University.

Bishop Hilliard has served widely in conferences and lectureships for ministers, including the Hampton University Ministers' Conference; The Oxford Round Table, Harris Manchester

College; and The National Working Group at Yale Divinity School. In this volume Bishop Hilliard offers his reflections and advice as they pertain to the purpose and the pursuit of church growth in the African American context. Although the subject at hand cannot possibly be exhausted in a single volume, both pastor and laity should be able to bear witness to a measurable increase in understanding why and how the church should grow.

—Christopher M. Jones,
editorial assistant to Bishop Donald Hilliard Jr.

PART ONE

✖ ✖ ✖ ✖ ✖ ✖

fundamentals for a
growing church

1. understanding church growth

Over the past twenty years a significant change has occurred in the dynamic of African American church life: the emergence of the "megachurch." Prior to about 1980 the phenomenon of a local church with a membership in the thousands—though increasingly common in the Bible Belt—was not a trend in the African American Christian community. In those days a black church with 500 members was considered a large church; a church of 1,000 or more was *huge*. When I came to the Second Baptist Church (Perth Amboy, New Jersey) in 1983, however, although our membership was 125, I was assured in my own soul that I had what black preachers call "a major house." The average church in America—black, white, or otherwise—had 85 to 125 members, a statistic that still holds true today, the increasing number of megachurches notwithstanding. Nevertheless, the recent appearance of black megachurches is forcing African American Christians to adjust their thinking about their churches and to reexamine what it means to grow.

It is important for me to be clear here. I am not one who believes that *mega* necessarily means "major" or "relevant." Thousands of small-to-average-size churches are faithfully doing ministry and making a difference. Whether we are talking about traditional mainline churches, such as the historic Abyssinian Baptist Church in Harlem, New York, and Ebenezer Baptist Church in Atlanta, or nontraditional churches like The Potter's House in Dallas and New Birth Cathedral in Lithonia, Georgia, megachurches today get the lion's share of attention at church-growth conferences precisely because of their size. And because of their seemingly explosive growth, they are often held up as role models to which all pastors and churches should aspire.

Part of the reason for this is the widely held assumption by most Americans that bigger is better. In our society a bigger house, a bigger car, and a bigger paycheck are all common earmarks of success and growth. Super-sized burgers and fries are better than the regular size. Corporations focus on increasing their "bottom line," often by hiring more people to produce and market more product to bring in more money. Clubs and service organizations are always after new members. Newspapers and magazines are always looking for new subscribers. In every case more people—whether employees, members, or clients/customers—means greater size and more money, both of which translate into *growth*.

Whenever we hear the word *growth*, we automatically think of increase in size and/or wealth, because that is the way our society and our educational system have taught us to think. We focus more on *quantitative* increase than on *qualitative* increase, partly because quantitative increase is easier to measure. Telling whether something is *bigger* than before is easy, but how do we tell whether it is *better*? How do we measure qualitative growth?

Unfortunately, this societal focus on quantitative growth has heavily influenced the way most American Christians evaluate their own as well as others' churches. When it comes to church growth, is bigger always better? Does one automatically lead to the other? What is the truest measure of church growth: getting bigger (quantitative) or getting better (qualitative)? Is it a combination of the two? Are they related?

Measuring Church Growth

Defining true and healthy church growth entails understanding the proper relationship between qualitative increase, which in the case of the church equates growth to *spiritual maturity*, and quantitative increase, which means both *numerical* and *financial* growth. Spiritual growth, numerical growth, and financial growth are not the same, nor are they interchangeable. Often, but not always, they are related. Spiritual growth in a church may or may not lead to numerical and financial growth, but numerical and financial growth by themselves will never lead to spiritual growth. Increases in numbers and wealth may make a church *bigger*, but apart from spiritual growth and relevant outreach, they do not necessarily make a church *better*.

Healthy churches are growing churches, but the key factor is *how* this growth is measured. Contrary to the assumption of many, a healthy, growing church cannot always be measured by greater numbers or a bigger budget. Healthy church growth is not always, nor is it even primarily, numerical. Just because the parking lot is full and you are welcoming new visitors every week does not automatically mean that your church is healthy or that it is growing. The Christian church is a local community of baptized believers and followers of Jesus Christ bound together by a common vision and called to proclaim Christ to a lost world and in his name minister to the needs of the sick, the poor, and those who are in need. Any group of people that does not function in this manner is not acting as a church no matter what they may call themselves. You can get a whole lot of people together, call yourselves a church, and yet not *be* a church. You can have a multi-million-dollar budget and still not be growing. You can carry on dozens of programs and still be ineffective. Again, healthy church growth cannot be defined by numbers and dollars alone.

Demonstrating Spiritual Maturity

Often, however, a correlation exists between the spiritual, numerical, and financial aspects of a growing church. In defining church growth, we must consider first the spiritual maturity of the people in the church. Are we growing in the grace, wisdom, and likeness of Christ? Are we demonstrating on an increasing basis love, personal holiness, piety, and the fullness of the Spirit of God in our lives? Do we exhibit an ever-expanding knowledge and understanding of the Word of God and sound doctrine? Are we translating our knowledge into compassionate acts of ministry and service to the needy around us? Do our words and our lives bear positive witness to the life-transforming and saving power of Jesus Christ? Do we bear witness to the fruit of a consecrated lifestyle? Regrettably, many churches these days are descending to preaching a crossless faith where the focus is too often on wealth and not on, as Dr. Gardner C. Taylor suggests, "an authentic understanding of the Gospel."[1]

If a church is spiritually sick, any so-called "growth" it experiences will be sick also. No amount of money or steady influx of new members can compensate if a church has the wrong spiritual focus. What good is it for a church to double or triple in size if it is headed in the wrong direction? What good is it for a church to have amassed large amounts of money in the bank if it is out of touch with God's will and purpose?

Spiritual health is the key factor for any church that desires to experience positive and lasting growth. Numerical and financial growth are significant primarily as they relate to and are reflections of a church's overall spiritual health. For this reason, the spiritual dimension of church growth will be the primary focus of this book. Spiritually healthy churches usually (but not always) experience numerical increase as a result of the life of the Spirit lived openly, honestly, and lovingly among a body of believers. These infectious qualities attract people. Relevant and practical ministry—another marker of a spiritually healthy church—also draws in new people. New people bring in new money, and so the church grows financially as well.

"De-stressing" Pastors

Unfortunately, the "bigger is better" mentality in America has left many Christians, including pastors, with an unhealthy or unrealistic expectation of church growth. The trend of continually holding up a few megachurches as models for emulation has only added to the problem. Of course, when a church such as Willow

Creek Community Church in South Barrington, Illinois, or World Changers Church International in College Park, Georgia, shows exponential growth, it is only natural to want to know why. How did they do it? What is the secret to their growth and success? What methods and programs did they use to attract so many people?

After all, what conscientious pastor does not want to see his or her church grow? Let's be honest: who among us hasn't harbored a hidden desire to be at the helm of our own "major" ministry or of some other church whose growth and success we admire? Realistically, however, not every church can or should become a megachurch. Churches do not arise in cookie-cutter fashion, identical in every way no matter their location or specific circumstances. One size does *not* fit all.

Nevertheless, unrealistic growth expectations imposed by congregations, denominational leadership, or even by individuals' own mistaken notions continue to subject many pastors to undue pressure to perform, to demonstrate measurable "success" in the form of large increases both in members and in tithes and offerings. As a result, an increasing number of pastors are becoming seriously stressed. Some burn out or become depressed because they have been unable to tap into the megachurch experience for themselves and the churches they serve. Overwhelmed with guilt and discouragement over their perceived failure and inadequacy, many are even leaving the ministry.

It is a tragic state of affairs when gifted leaders are lost from the church because they failed to meet a false and misleading standard of growth and success, whether self-imposed or imposed from the outside. When it comes to church growth, size is not everything; it is not even the most important thing. As noted above, quantifying a megachurch numerically does not qualify it as being a "major" church or a healthy one despite its large size and affluent bank account. At the same time, there are thousands of churches that are spiritually strong and that serve God faithfully every day yet remain modest both in size and in financial resources.

Quite often, depression and discouragement of pastors over their perceived failure to bring growth to their churches is the direct result of focusing on an erroneous standard for measuring and evaluating that growth. Many of these pastors beat themselves up for no reason. The vast majority of American churches fall into the small-to-medium category, and most of them are located in small-town and rural settings. For most of these churches, the likelihood of their ever attaining megachurch status is extremely small—and perhaps this is what is meant to be. The same is true for most urban and inner-city African American churches.

The megachurch phenomenon is just that—a *phenomenon*. It is not the norm and never has been. This is the witness of two thousand years of global church history as well as the history of church life in America. Throughout history, the work of the kingdom of God has been carried out by local fellowships of believers that were for the most part small in size and often limited in resources.

Just because a pastor labors faithfully for years in a church without seeing much numerical or financial increase does not mean he or she has failed. Neither does it call into question a pastor's calling, commitment, or anointing. Jesus Christ is the head of his body, the church. As the head of the church, Jesus has a specific will for each body of believers, one that varies from body to body. While the basic commission of the church is universal— to make disciples of all nations and baptize them in the name of the Father, Son, and Holy Spirit (Matthew 28:19)—the specific approach to fulfilling that commission varies from one local church body to the next.

The reasons for this are simple: no two local church fellowships are exactly alike, and Jesus equips each church for its specific assignment. For example, at any given time, one church's primary assignment might be to reach students, while another is placed and equipped for an effective ministry to drug addicts. A church's location as well as its specific assignment influences its particular growth pattern.

For this reason, pastor, it is extremely important for you to discern the will of God for your own church. One of the greatest dangers to church health and growth is when a church compares itself with another church and ends up feeling invalid and inadequate because it doesn't "measure up" to that other church in terms of membership, financial resources, or varieties and types of ministries offered. What is right for one church may not be right for yours. You may be called of God to pastor a small congregation, which is just as high and great a calling as the call to lead the largest megachurch. The call is the same; only your specific assignment differs. The key is to know and do the will of God for your church. If you follow God's will, there is no reason to become stressed or depressed by apparent lack of numerical and financial growth. You can believe that God will bring the increase in the right time and in the right manner.

Understanding Your Motivation

"*Why* do we want to grow?" is a question every pastor and church that seek growth need to ask. Appearances are one thing; motivation is another. Motivation is a key factor in determining whether or not a church will experience healthy growth. Our appearance-conscious culture tends to focus on externals only, and many churches have fallen into that same trap. God takes a different perspective, one that is more concerned with the inner issues of the human heart. In other words, God focuses on our motivation: "For the LORD does not see as mortals see; they look on the outward appearance, but the LORD looks on the heart" (1 Samuel 16:7, NRSV).

Pastor, why do you want your church to grow? Do you want to keep up with a successful church in your area by imitating it so you can have what they have and do what they do? Are you trying to build a reputation in your city as a powerful "mover and shaker" in the Christian community? Do you seek validation for your ministry and believe you will find it in a bigger budget, bigger buildings, and a bigger congregation? Do you crave the admiration and approval of others? Are you under pressure from your deacons, elders, congregation, or denominational leadership to produce tangible and measurable "growth" in your church? Or do you simply believe that bigger is better? These are just a few examples of the kinds of unhealthy motivational traps that pastors and churches frequently fall into when striving to grow.

On the other hand, do you see church growth as a by-product of fulfilling Christ's Great Commission to "make disciples of all the nations" (Matthew 28:19)? Does church growth mean to you watching more and more church members grow into spiritually mature and discipled believers who are filled with the Holy Spirit, knowledgeable about the Word of God, and active in compassionate, meaningful ministry to the hurting and needy? Do you want your church to grow because you desire to be obedient to the Lord and to carry out God's will? Do you value larger numbers in your church primarily as a marker of how effective your church is at reaching people for Christ rather than just an indicator that you are "bigger" than you were? All of these represent healthy spiritual motivations for growth that come from the heart and are planted there by God.

Differentiating between Motivation and Inspiration

In reality, healthy church growth is not so much a matter of motivation only but of *inspiration*. Motivation stems from either an outside stimulus or a drive that comes from our own strength or resources. Inspiration, on the other hand, has its origin in God. The word *inspire* literally means to "breathe into," as when God breathed into Adam the breath of life and he became a living being (Genesis 2:7) or when God "breathed" the words of the Scriptures into the hearts and minds of the writers of the Bible (2 Timothy 3:16).

True and healthy church growth is *always* initiated by God. It is a work of the Holy Spirit as the Lord Jesus exercises his headship over his body in order to mold his people into his likeness. Churches that experience genuine and lasting growth are those that determinedly position themselves to hear the Lord's voice and to obey the leading of his Spirit. Human-motivated efforts may bring about apparent growth. Such "growth," however, is usually short-lived. Rarely is it permanent. Anything achieved by human effort must be sustained by human effort, and human effort is finite. The psalmist has declared that "unless the LORD builds the house, they who build it labor in vain" (Psalm 127:1). We humans grow tired, become distracted, and get discouraged, and those things that we are shoring up in our own strength begin to sag and eventually collapse. The problem with motivation is that it has to be applied and reapplied continually because it comes from a finite source. Inspiration, however, can sustain us indefinitely because it derives from the infinite resources of God.

A church should periodically reexamine its motivations for growth. This is especially true today because there are so many unhealthy examples for a church to imitate. As I stated earlier, if we are after numbers or money alone, we are after the wrong thing.

Adopting a Biblical Model for Church Growth

Comparing one church to another is dangerous and almost always disheartening, especially for the church that seems to come up short in the comparison. And because the vast majority of churches are small or medium in size, holding up the contemporary megachurch as the model for what a church ought to be is both unfair and unrealistic. Where then do we look for a healthy model of church growth?

For me, there is no better model than the one found in the second chapter of Acts. Beginning on the day of Pentecost, the New Testament church experienced phenomenal growth that continued for many years until it had spread throughout the Roman

Empire. This biblical model is simple yet profoundly powerful. It is the church model I have used with great success in my own ministry. Luke the physician, the writer of the Book of Acts, describes the growth and influence of the early church this way:

> And they continued steadfastly in the apostles' doctrine and fellowship, in the breaking of bread, and in prayers. Then fear came upon every soul, and many wonders and signs were done through the apostles. Now all who believed were together, and had all things in common, and sold their possessions and goods, and divided them among all, as anyone had need. So continuing daily with one accord in the temple, and breaking bread from house to house, they ate their food with gladness and simplicity of heart, praising God and having favor with all the people. And the Lord added to the church daily those who were being saved.
> —Acts, 2:42-47

The following chapters will examine this model in greater detail, but let's take a brief overview to get a picture of what the early church was like and how it grew. From this passage of Scripture we learn that the early church was:

a church of sound preaching and teaching: "they continued steadfastly in the apostles' doctrine"

a church of community: "they continued steadfastly in . . . fellowship, [and] in the breaking of bread"

a church of prayer: "they continued steadfastly in . . . prayers"

a church of power: "many wonders and signs were done through the apostles"

a church of compassion: "all who believed were together, and had all things in common, and sold their possessions and goods, and divided them among all, as anyone had need" *a church of unity:* "continuing daily with one accord"

a church of joy: "they ate their food with gladness and simplicity of heart"

a church of worship: "praising God"

a church of good reputation: "having favor with all the people"

a church that trusted God for the increase: "the Lord added to the church daily those who were being saved."

A healthy, growing church will exhibit all of these characteristics to one degree or another. While all of these elements are important, I want to emphasize the last one: *a church that trusted God for the increase.* Whatever else we do, we must remember that it is God who brings the growth, not us. Unless the Lord brings the increase, all of our efforts at growth ultimately will be vain and futile.

2. preparing for growth

⊠ ⊠ ⊠ ⊠ ⊠ ⊠

Our generation has witnessed in general a great decline in the inward reality of the Christian faith for many believers. Today an increasing tendency in many churches is to stress merely the outward appearance, to focus only on the external trappings of "religion." Even our prayer lives tend to concentrate more on what we can see, touch, feel, and do instead of on what God can do or who we can be in God. Yet the Lord is calling all who will hear to rediscover and return to the inward reality of the Christian faith, to earnestly seek the living God. We who are faithful must discipline ourselves and sensitize our spirits to hear God's voice so that we may know the divine will and way. This is an indispensable prerequisite for healthy church growth.

Regaining Our Focus

To regain inner spiritual focus and prepare ourselves for the growth God wants to bring, we must adopt and nurture three attitudes in our hearts: *humility*, *hunger*, and *hope*.

Humility If we want our churches to grow, we must first come before God in a spirit of humility. We read in 1 Peter 5:6: "Humble yourselves under the mighty hand of God, that He may exalt you in due time." When we humble ourselves before God, we can take a good hard look at ourselves and reexamine our own character and our own personal issues. God brings to light the things we need to work on.

This is important because periodically we need to be reminded who we are and where we came from. No matter how appealing our apparel may be or how extravagant our houses and cars, we all are merely flesh and blood human beings who need God.

We hurt. We bleed. We experience fear and insecurity. As much as anybody else, we need to know the presence, the love, the grace, and the mercy of God.

We often get so caught up in what we put *on* ourselves that we forget that God is more concerned with what we put *in* ourselves. God is much more interested in who we are inside than in what we wear outside. Our inner nature and character determine our outward manner and the way we treat other people. One of the reasons why some people don't turn to God is because they see us, the children of God, acting in an arrogant and puffed-up manner. We become so blessed that we forget our humble beginnings. If we are not careful, our blessings will bless us right out of the spirit of godly humility, and we will start looking down on those who don't have what we have or who have not attained the education that we have attained.

When that happens, we forget who and what the church is supposed to be in the first place. The church becomes more of a country club than a church, more of an exclusive clique than an inclusive fellowship where the broken and the bruised can be healed, the hungry can be fed, the lonely can find friends, and all can come to know Christ.

And therein lies the challenge. We must never forget that we are called to identify with those who do not have as much as we do. There is nothing wrong with having fancy clothes, nice cars, or plenty of money, but a problem arises when we become prideful and place ourselves in a category above others. If a church wants to grow, it must begin with a commitment to humility.

Hunger A proper attitude of humility toward God will stir in us the second attitude necessary for growth: a hunger for God. Everyone needs food to grow, but we won't eat unless we're hungry. It is the same way with our spirit. Jesus says in Matthew 5:6, "Blessed are those who hunger and thirst for righteousness, for they shall be filled." We need to be hungry for God—for God's

Word, God's will, God's perspective and guidance, God's peace, and God's truth. In short, we need to be hungry for all the things God desires.

Hope Attitudes of humility and spiritual hunger lead to the third attitude—hope—because we are looking to a God we can trust and depend on. The apostle Paul wrote to the church in Rome about the power of hope:

> Having been justified by faith, we have peace with God through our Lord Jesus Christ, through whom also we have access by faith into this grace in which we stand, and rejoice in hope of the glory of God. And not only that, but we also glory in tribulations, knowing that tribulation produces perseverance; and perseverance, character; and character, hope. Now hope does not disappoint, because the love of God has been poured out in our hearts by the Holy Spirit who was given to us.
> —Romans 5:1-5

Everyone needs hope. Just as food is essential for the health and survival of the human body, hope is essential for the health and survival of the human spirit. We human beings can survive the loss of almost anything except hope. As we come before God in humility and hunger, we need hope to fill and empower our spirits. Hope enables us to look beyond our present circumstances with confidence, knowing that whatever we see before us, no matter what "it" is, "it" does not change who God is. God is still God! We may not know what tomorrow holds, but hope assures us that God holds tomorrow. This kind of hope is not wishful thinking but steadfast assurance based on the integrity and promise of God.

These three attitudes—humility *toward* God, hunger *for* God, and hope *in* God—prepare us for growth because they orient our thinking so that we acknowledge our total dependence on God to bring the increase we desire. As we align our will with God's will and surrender all our plans and methods and ways to a holy way, God will work in and through us to bring about the growth God wants for us not only as individuals but also corporately as local church bodies.

Now that we have defined healthy church growth and examined some of the conditions under which that growth occurs, it is time to turn our attention to the essential foundations for healthy, lasting church growth.

Serving the Lord Faithfully

One characteristic all healthy, growing churches have in common is a commitment to serving the Lord faithfully. Joshua told the Israelites, "As for me and my house, we will serve the LORD" (Joshua 24:15). Even though Joshua was talking about his own family, his words apply just as much to the church because the church is a family: the family of God. As individuals as well as a corporate body, we must be committed to serving the Lord with all our hearts. Heartfelt service to God will require three things of us.

First, we will need to be *deliberate*. This means making conscious, reasoned decisions and purposeful, intentional choices. We must be deliberate in making our churches what God wants them to be. We must be deliberate in prayer for our families, our churches, our neighborhoods, our communities, and our nation.

We must be deliberate in preaching and teaching the Word of God as well as the doctrines of the Christian faith. Our children will never learn these things and live them in their generation unless we teach them. Hit-or-miss learning opportunities will not suffice. Repetition is the best teacher. One intentional method we used for training our youth recently was an overnight "Youth Prayer Shut-in," in which our youth were given lessons on the basics of the Christian faith. We must be deliberate about feeding the Word of God regularly to our children as well as to ourselves.

We must be deliberate in teaching and demonstrating order, both in the church and in the home. We live in a day when many people have no concept of legitimate authority and therefore no respect for it. Teaching our children to respect parental and civil authority can help them learn to respect and honor God. The reverse is also true: teaching them to respect and honor God will instill in them respect for other legitimate authority in their lives. Without order there is bound to be confusion, and confusion can lead to destruction.

We must be deliberate about passing our faith on to our children. If they are to be the world-changers of their generation, we must instill in them the faith that has made a difference in our lives: a passionate love for Jesus and an unshakable hope in him as the Light of the world.

Second, we must be *determined*. Being deliberate means making a conscious decision; being determined involves follow-through. The moment we make a conscious decision to serve the Lord, the enemy will go all out to distract or deter us. The devil fears nothing more than Christian people committed to prayer and to the Word of God and determined to serve God no matter what. Satan is no match for that kind of power. I recommend keeping 1 Peter 5:6-11 close to your heart as you reflect on such matters. Godly determination can resist the power of satanic attack.

Nevertheless, we must be wary or we will fail. We must be determined to love one another, lift up one another in prayer, encourage one another, and make ourselves accountable to one another. After all, there is strength in numbers. There is no such thing as an only child in the kingdom of God. We need mutual support to keep one another strong and walking in truth as the light and salt of the earth. At the Cathedral we strongly believe in accountability. Whether one serves in the capacity of ordained clergy or lay ministry, one must submit an "accountability form" to the appropriate authority when he or she is unable to carry out a specific responsibility. The idea is to foster honesty, integrity, and accountability within a faith community. Yes, we need each other to stay strong. We also need each other to remain transparent to keep potential spiritual hindrances from disconnecting a unified spiritual body.

Finally, we must be *demonstrative*. We must not be afraid to show our love for one another. If people outside the church see us who are in the church freely loving each other in godly love, they will be drawn to the church, because that kind of love is unknown in the nonbelieving world. We must also be demonstrative in the way we stand up for what we believe and the way we put our faith into action. One common accusation that unbelievers make against the church is that it is full of hypocrites. While accusations will always be made against the church by misinformed people, we must endeavor to be genuine redemptive people. While there is no perfect church, we must nevertheless strive to be genuine.

Paul's counsel to Titus applies to us as well: "Likewise, exhort the young men to be sober-minded, in all things showing yourself to be a pattern of good works; in doctrine showing integrity, reverence, incorruptibility, sound speech that cannot be condemned, that one who is an opponent may be ashamed, having nothing evil to say of you" (Titus 2:7-8). Paul is talking here about demonstrative faith: not just a bunch of pretty, pious words but faith demonstrated in action.

Setting a High Standard

The church belongs to Jesus Christ. He is the head of the church and has absolute authority over it. It is he who has set the standard, and we must work to meet it. A church that wishes to grow must be willing to work consistently and continually to meet Christ's high standard of excellence. A church will be successful in this endeavor only to the degree that every person in the church body is committed to the standard. If anyone is not committed to the common standard, the body as a whole will suffer.

In practical terms setting a high standard means first of all that we must be *prepared* for God to move in our church the way that God wants to move. We have to be willing to let go of the "controls." This is especially true for pastors and others in leadership. It means hiring people who are capable of operating with excellence and paying them according to their skill set and experience. I have found Stan Toler and Alan Nelson's book *The Five Star Church: Serving God and His People with Excellence* (Regal Books) to be a valuable resource.

We must also be prepared for spiritual warfare by dressing daily in the whole armor of God as described in Ephesians 6:10-18: the belt of truth, the breastplate of righteousness, the shoes of the gospel of peace, the shield of faith, the helmet of salvation, and the sword of the Spirit, which is the Word of God. We cannot fight the enemy with hearsay. Only the truth that we have made our own by faith is sufficient for us to win such battles.

Second, we need to have God's *perspective* on every issue. Everything we say and do should reflect God's perspective and priorities. We must be concerned about the things God is concerned about. We learn God's perspective by reading, studying, and meditating on the Word; praying; and paying attention to the needs of the people we serve. In other words, we learn God's perspective by spending time in God's presence.

Third—and I cannot emphasize this enough—we must be a people of *prayer*. As the people of God, we need to be well instructed and become thoroughly experienced in all kinds of prayer, including petition, supplication, and intercession. Prayer is the church's lifeline. Through prayer the church can overcome the enemy, influence civic leaders and public officials at every level, and even alter the course of history. Prayer is powerful. Prayer changes things. Prayer can bring healing to a sick person and bring a sinner to repentance. Poet Alfred, Lord Tennyson wrote, "More things are wrought by prayer than this world dreams of." Jesus said, "If two of you agree on earth concerning anything that they ask, it will be done for them by My Father in heaven" (Matthew 18:19). Persistent, faithful prayer helps prevent the enemy from gaining a foothold in our hearts and in our churches.

Fourth, in addition to being a people of prayer, we must be a *prophetic* people, not just individually but corporately as well. I'm not talking primarily about personal prophetic utterances given under the inspiration of the Holy Spirit—although that is part of what it means to prophesy—but about prophesying in the larger sense, which means to proclaim a message. In our calling to proclaim Christ to the world, all of us are prophets. A prophetic church boldly engages and confronts the secular culture and speaks the truth of God that runs counter to that culture. This is the church's mission, and we must not shy away from it. We are called to be a voice for the voiceless and powerless.

Fifth, the church should be a people of *praise*, a people who are not afraid to worship the Lord in spirit and truth and with reckless abandon. We should always be ready to "enter into His gates with thanksgiving, and into His courts with praise" (Psalm 100:4). Praise and worship should be as natural to us as breathing. We should know how to reverence God, know when God is calling for reverential silence, and know when there is a need for a war cry. For example, last year marked an unprecedented number of deaths in our congregation because of cancer. The experience was heartwrenching to me as a pastor. Not only did I call for church-wide prayer every Wednesday morning at 5:30—the war cry—but I invited doctors and research specialists to give presentations on the issue of cancer in the African American community. I called for seminars related to healthcare. The church must be both spiritual and practical in its approach to such issues. Some ailments can be combated by people armed with information. We must not overspiritualize everything. A responsible pastor will inform his or her flock on when to cry out or remain silent in the presence of the Lord.

Sixth, we must be a church of *provision*. We have an obligation before God to provide for the needs of the "temple" through an honest, sincere, and whole tithe, to support the ministries of the church with our offerings, and to provide for the needs of the hungry and the naked and those who are in trouble. This "obligation" is something we should fulfill freely, willingly, and with great joy, remembering the Lord's abundant blessings and favor toward us. Just as God has blessed us, we are called to bless others.

Seventh, we need people who subordinate *personality* to the will of God. That is, we are not to allow our personalities or personal desires to take precedence over what God wants to do. It also means putting the needs, desires, and welfare of others in the church above our own. Paul says: "Let nothing be done through selfish ambition or conceit, but in lowliness of mind let each esteem others better than himself. Let each of you look out not only for his own interests, but also for the interests of others" (Philippians 2:3-4). What Paul is talking about here, of course, is humility.

Finally, a growing church is a church of *power*. Before Jesus ascended into heaven he promised his disciples, "But you shall receive power when the Holy Spirit has come upon you; and you shall be witnesses to Me in Jerusalem, and in all Judea and Samaria, and to the end of the earth" (Acts 1:8). That power is always available to us, but we must learn to tap into it regularly and consistently. As Jesus said in John 15:5, he is the vine, we are the branches, and without him we can do nothing. We must not allow ourselves to rot on the vine. Instead, we must abide in him, individually and corporately, and allow him to produce abundant fruit.

Being Willing to Take Risks

One reason many churches fail to grow is because the pastor, the other church leaders, or both, are unwilling to take a risk. Growing churches are risk-taking churches, not in an impetuous or foolhardy way, but in a willingness to try something new, to move in a direction they have never gone before, to step out in faith to pursue a vision even if current circumstances indicate otherwise. For example, the Cathedral International initially sought to secure twenty-five acres to build a new edifice for worship. When the executive cabinet of pastors and elders located land in Cranbury, New Jersey, they discovered that there existed one hundred acres for purchase. Since I believed that this opportunity for purchase was divinely orchestrated, I voted to purchase the entire plot. Please hear me. I did not know at the time whether we could purchase the twenty-five acres, yet I moved on the one hundred acres. Not only did God find funding for the entire plot of land, but the landowners donated fifty acres on their own. We received funding to build on one hundred acres, fifty of which were given to us free! Be a risk taker! Risk taking, however, means moving out onto the cutting edge of ministry and staying there no matter what. Thinking outside the box, stepping out of your comfort zone—whatever you call it, growth always involves an element of risk.

The danger in all of this is that we tend to take fewer risks as we get older. As leaders or churches enter "middle age," we must be especially careful not to lose our cutting-edge approach to ministry. Our message never changes—Jesus Christ is the same yesterday, today, and forever (Hebrews 13:8)—but our methods and manner of proclaiming that message, as well as our approach to ministry, must always be changing and adapting so that we can continue to reach people and speak to them where they are. Churches that want to grow must be willing to take some risks, and the pastor must take the lead.

How do you grow a church? Build your church by building the people in the church, and then let them grow the church. Our job as pastors is to shepherd the people, to keep our vision fresh, and to preach, teach, and reach. A key part of these three words is *each*. Effective pr*each*ing, t*each*ing and r*each*ing in a growing church aim to touch *each* person who comes in contact with its ministry.

3. foundations for healthy church growth

☒ ☒ ☒ ☒ ☒ ☒

No one-size-fits-all plan or program for church growth exists that will work in every church everywhere. In today's results-oriented environment, it is easy for us pastors and church leaders to slip into the "bandwagon syndrome"—trying something in our church simply because it worked in somebody else's church. Then, when we fail to see the results we expected, we are disappointed and discouraged. We wonder what went wrong.

Maybe nothing went wrong. Perhaps the plan failed simply because it was not suited for your church. Another church might have used the plan successfully because certain elements or conditions necessary for its success were present there that were absent in your situation. This is not necessarily a bad thing. It merely indicates that each church is unique. Each has its own environment, personality, conditions, and circumstances. Whether a particular church-growth plan or program is right for your church is a question that must be answered through much prayer and careful study.

Church growth does not just happen; a church must prepare itself to grow. Certainly the divine favor of the Lord is a critical factor in a church's growth, but God's favor rests on churches that have proven faithful to prepare themselves by giving proper attention to the fundamentals. Anyone who desires to build a successful structure, whether a house or a skyscraper, must begin by laying a sound foundation. Church growth is no different. A church that desires to grow must give care to laying the kind of solid biblical foundation that will put it in a position to grow. Without a proper foundation, healthy growth is impossible. Jesus stressed the importance of laying the right foundation:

Therefore whoever hears these sayings of Mine, and
does them, I will liken him to a wise man who built his
house on the rock: and the rain descended, the floods
came, and the winds blew and beat on that house; and
it did not fall, for it was founded on the rock. But everyone who hears these sayings of Mine, and does not do
them, will be like a foolish man who built his house on
the sand: and the rain descended, the floods came, and
the winds blew and beat on that house; and it fell. And
great was its fall.
—Matthew 7:24-27

While each church is unique, certain foundational elements are
necessary for every church that desires to grow. In this chapter
we will look at ten foundational elements.

Vision

The first foundational element of a church that desires to grow is
vision. Every church needs a clear vision; otherwise it has no idea
where it is going or how it is going to get there. A church that
lacks vision, if it survives at all, will likely dissipate its energy and
resources on plans and programs that have no relation either to
each other or to the true ministry and mission fields of the church.
Without a clear vision, a church will tend to fall into either the
"bandwagon syndrome" ("Let's try this because everybody else is
doing it") or the "cafeteria syndrome" ("Let's try a little of this
and a little of that; oh, and let's get some of this over here").

Proverbs 29:18 says, "Where there is no vision, the people perish" (KJV). The same verse in the New King James Version reads,
"Where there is no revelation, the people cast off restraint."
Although the wording is slightly different, the meaning is the
same. A church that lacks vision, that has no clear revelation
from God as to its direction, will perish because it will never fulfill its purpose for being. The people will "cast off restraint" as

they pursue one program or idea after another with no plan or unifying vision to bring cohesion.

Normally, the pastor is the "front person," the "pacesetter," the one entrusted with the vision. Unless the pastor has a clear vision from the Lord, and unless he or she sets that vision before the people and keeps it before them, the church will not grow. For this reason, pastors who want to see their churches grow must be clear on their call to ministry, confident in the direction they want to lead their churches, and circumspect in their personal walk God.

It would be hard to overestimate the importance of a pastor's personal lifestyle on the health and growth of a church. I know this from personal experience. When I first became pastor more than twenty years ago of what was then called Second Baptist Church, I, like most new pastors, encountered some opposition. Some of the opposition was aimed at me directly, but most of it was opposition to God. Certain elements in the church were opposed to the Word of God and to God's truth. As it turned out, this opposition worked to my benefit because it kept me on my toes.

One of the ways I handled the opposition was to try to make sure that I had my *i*'s dotted and my *t*'s crossed in my personal life. I had to be very careful to practice personal holiness. Prayer was my lifeline, and the Word of God truly was my daily bread. I even fasted twice a week because I needed to make sure that my personal life was in order before God as well as before people. I sought to always be prepared before I stood in the pulpit. First, I studied the biblical text thoroughly to make sure I had a word from the Lord. I try never to preach "from the hip." Next, I tried to practice what I preached. Finally, the policies and programs of the church evolved from the preaching.

There, in a nutshell, is my prescription for pastors who want to prepare their churches to grow. It all begins with *us*. Before God can give us a clear vision for our church, we must prepare the fertile soil of our personal lives. We must give careful attention and care to our prayer life, our preaching, and our programs—in that order. Our prayer life comes first. Our preaching grows out of our prayer life just as our programs should be an outgrowth of our preaching. For example, if we preach that the Lord can deliver people from drug and alcohol addiction, then our church needs to have a program that will help people do just that—a program that will help addicts and alcoholics come to faith in Christ, face their personal and societal demons, and find deliverance.

In short, the programs in our church should tie in with our preaching. Our preaching should be an outgrowth of the divine power and anointing that should be on our own lives as a result of our consistent walk with the Lord. And all of this should be inspired and driven by the personal vision God has given us.

The vision we set before the people should challenge them to press forward and should change their personal lives. They should begin thinking at higher levels, thinking "out of the box." They should be thinking spiritually, thinking financially, thinking about the future and about the direction of their families and their church. Such "forward" thinking is a powerful and important key for church growth. Churches with a clear vision set higher personal and corporate standards of excellence and holiness than do churches that have no vision. Whenever a church follows its vision, it enjoys the favor of God, and the vision helps the church walk in unity. And unity is a strong stimulant for growth.

Visionary churches tend to have visionary pastors. Most visionary pastors, like most visionaries in general, think in the abstract. We see what God is getting ready to do, but we can't always articulate it. That is why it is important for the abstract to be balanced by the concrete. A visionary pastor needs a leader to come alongside him or her who thinks in the concrete, a business-minded person or someone gifted in organizational or administrative areas to help anchor the vision and bring balance. A pastor may see a vision that will cost $100,000, while the leadership knows that all they have is $25,000. That is, the pastor may say, "This is what I want to do," and the leaders may say, "Well, this is what you have to work with."

The point here is balance, not the diluting of the vision. Visionaries are usually ready to move on the vision right away; the concrete thinkers help them to recognize the practical details that must be worked out before the vision can come to pass and to acknowledge that this may take some time. At the same time, however, don't let the reality of your situation steal your vision. One of the biggest challenges in bringing and keeping a vision before the people is teaching them that just because something is not in the budget today does not mean God will not provide for it tomorrow. Pastor, don't lose heart when the dollars and cents reality does not match your vision. *Wherever there is vision, God gives provision.*

Over the years our church has owned many different properties. At one point we owned fourteen at one time. In every instance, whenever we began pursuing a piece of property or sought to construct a building, we never had all the money we needed when we started. Without exception, as we followed our vision, God provided. When we were preparing to purchase and refurbish the building that houses the Cathedral International today, our bank denied our loan request. They felt that our church, as large as it was even then, lacked the wherewithal to handle a $2.5 million project, even though we were only asking for a loan of less than half that amount. We proceeded with our plans anyway. God was faithful—already working things out. By the time we would have needed the bank's money, we had already received that amount through tithes and offerings.

My point is simply this: Don't let your vision be confined by current circumstances that make it appear impossible. As visionary pastors and leaders, we must have the courage of our convictions and the determination to stay the course until the vision comes to pass! If we are going to lead people, we have to give clear guidance, sometimes declaring, "This is the way it must be."

That is one reason we pastors need to be clear and secure in our call to ministry. In order to lead, we must know by whose ultimate authority we are called to pastor the church. A congregation may have called us or a board or a bishop may have assigned us, but ultimately, *God* is the One who has placed us where we are. Our authority, while validated by the people, comes from God.

In addition to this spiritual authority, we need moral authority. Our moral authority will depend on the integrity of our character and lifestyle. While all of us have issues that need to be worked on, we should aim with all diligence to "walk the talk."

In Habakkuk the Lord says, "Write the vision and make it plain on tablets, that he may run who reads it" (2:2). Pastor, what vision has the Lord given you for your church? Where has God placed your church, and what has God equipped you to do in your area? Proclaim the vision in the authority and boldness of the Holy Spirit, and keep it before the people.

The Centrality of Christ

Another foundational truth for church growth is that a growing church must be committed to the absolute *centrality of Christ* in its preaching, teaching, and ministry—indeed, in all of church life. Acts 2:42 says, "They [the church] continued steadfastly in the apostles' doctrine." And what was foremost in the apostles' doctrine? Jesus Christ—his life, death, resurrection, and certain return. He is the Son of God and God in human flesh. He is also the head of the church, which is his body (Ephesians 1:22-23, 5:23). Simon Peter said of Jesus, "Nor is there salvation in any other, for there is no other name under heaven given among men by which we must be saved" (Acts 4:12). The apostle Paul also expressed this Christ-centered focus, writing, "We preach Christ crucified" (1 Corinthians 1:23), and "I determined not to know anything among you except Jesus Christ and Him crucified" (1 Corinthians. 2:2). As head of the church, Jesus Christ is central to everything we are and do.

If Christ is central to the church, then church people ought to be Jesus people. Our lives are to be motivated by love for each other as well as for those outside the church. Indeed, it is by our love that others will see and come to know Christ. Jesus said: "A new commandment I give to you, that you love one another; as I have loved you, that you also love one another. By this all will know that you are My disciples, if you have love for one another" (John 13:34-35).

The witness of the early church and one of the key secrets to its phenomenal growth was that they loved each other. Acts 2:42 says that these early believers "continued steadfastly in . . . fellowship." Verse 46 adds that they were "continuing daily with one accord in the temple." Love is contagious. People all around us are starving for true love. We have become a "high-tech, low-touch" society. If we as believers would simply live in the spirit and truth of these verses, our church buildings would not be able to hold all the people who would come every week. Because of this witness of love and unity in the early church, "the Lord added to the church daily those who were being saved" (v. 47).

If we want our churches to grow, we need to be Jesus people who live as if we know Jesus. The only way we can really know Jesus is through our allowing him to be Savior and Lord, studying the Word, walking close to him daily, and keeping him as the central focus of all we do.

Biblical Preaching

Not only will a growing church have a clear and unified vision and a Christ-centered focus, but it will also be committed to preaching a complete, unified, and biblical gospel message. Too much teaching and preaching today is unbalanced. A complete message means preaching the *whole* Bible, avoiding the temptation to concentrate on a few pet themes or favorite Scriptures. Many churches are lopsided in their preaching, focusing only on a "prosperity" message or a "faith" message or on "signs and wonders." While we desperately need messages on prosperity, faith, and healing, these do not reflect the entire biblical message. Balanced biblical preaching takes in the entire biblical revelation and helps promote the development of biblically balanced believers in the church.

Preaching the gospel is the single most important activity we can do as a church. It is indeed at the center of the commission Christ gave to us when he said, "Go therefore and make disciples of all the nations, baptizing them in the name of the Father and of the Son and of the Holy Spirit, teaching them to observe all things that I have commanded you" (Matthew 28:19-20) and "Go into all the world and preach the gospel to every creature" (Mark 16:15).

The apostle Paul also stressed the central place of preaching in reaching lost people with the good news of Christ:

> How shall they call on Him in whom they have not believed? And how shall they believe in Him of whom they have not heard? And how shall they hear without a preacher? And how shall they preach unless they are sent? As it is written:
> > "How beautiful are the feet of those who preach the gospel of peace,
> > Who bring glad tidings of good things!"
> —Romans 10:14-15

Paul also charged his protégé Timothy, "Preach the word! Be ready in season and out of season. Convince, rebuke, exhort, with all longsuffering and teaching" (2 Timothy 4:2).

Many churches today, in an effort to be "relevant," have departed from biblical preaching in favor of philosophical messages or homilies drawn from current affairs or modern social science. While there is certainly nothing wrong with trying to remain relevant for our hearers, our preaching must first be biblical. Besides, there is nothing more relevant to modern society than the gospel of Christ preached honestly in the power and anointing of the Holy Spirit. Biblical preaching means preaching the *Bible*—the full biblical revelation of God.

Purposeful Prayer

Another foundational element for growth is for a church to be committed to purposeful prayer. This means learning to pray specifically and with conscious purpose rather than praying general prayers that are vague and open-ended. We need to pray specific prayers, whether for healing or deliverance, for direction and guidance, or for the need of a friend or loved one. James writes, "You do not have because you do not ask. You ask and do not receive, because you ask amiss, that you may spend it on your pleasures" (James 4:2-3). To "ask amiss" means to ask for the wrong thing or to ask for the wrong reason. Specific prayers help us stay focused on the right issues and give rise to specific answers. Jesus teaches, "Ask, and it will be given to you; seek, and you will find; knock, and it will be opened to you. For everyone who asks receives, and he who seeks finds, and to him who knocks it will be opened" (Matthew 7:7-8).

A growing church is a church that learns to pray specifically and with purpose. We need to pray specifically and consistently for church growth. We need to pray specifically for healing of the sick and for deliverance of those who are bound by drugs or alcohol, hopelessness, and despair. We need to pray specifically for those who have lost their jobs or suffered financial reversal. We need to pray specifically for the salvation of lost friends and loved ones. We need to pray specifically for people stuck in the quicksand of poverty. We need to pray specifically for our young men and women that they will not sell themselves cheap but preserve their minds and bodies in dignity and honor. We need to pray specifically for spiritual awakening and for moral and spiritual change in our neighborhoods and communities. This list could go on and on. My point is that churches that wish to grow must learn to pray specifically and with purpose.

Our church has prayer times literally every day. Several years ago I implemented a corporate policy mandating that all administrative staff begin their workday at 9:30 a.m. with a word of prayer. At noon each Wednesday, both the church staff and the community gather for noonday service, in which powerful prayer precedes a time of worship, praise, and preaching. The elders of the church coordinate prayer schedules with the deacons and ministers. The deacons and ministers, in turn, designate weekly prayer times to the laity to ensure that the entire church leadership remains committed to a spiritual life filled with daily prayer.

For the last few years we have called the church to an early morning prayer gathering on Wednesdays at 5:30 and 6:30 a.m. with amazing results. Small prayer teams have been formed and charged to pray for the church on twenty-four-hour rotations. While these prayer teams remain small in number, under the leading of the Holy Spirit, they function with incredible power. And we have been transformed in the process.

We have learned that as a result of our commitment to prayer, we can expect not only spiritual growth, but numerical growth, as the needs of the community are met through the ministry of prayer. Through unrelenting petitions to God for peace, health, and prosperity in the land, the entire community thrives and the church grows.

Dynamic Worship

Another foundation stone found in virtually every growing church is dynamic, powerful worship. In the church of the Book of Acts, the believers were "praising God and having favor with all the people. And the Lord added to the church daily those who were being saved" (Acts 2:47). This verse makes it clear that the quality of the early church's worship ("praising God") was one of the factors contributing to its phenomenal growth.

Heartfelt, Spirit-filled worship is a catalyst for growth because it ushers people into a deeper experience of God's presence. Worship brings us closer to God. Psalm 22:3 says that God is "holy, enthroned in the praises of Israel." The King James Version for this verse says that God "inhabitest" the praises of people. Whenever the church gathers for worship, God is there in our midst. Churches that regularly experience the presence of God in a powerful way attract people who are hungry for a genuine encounter with God.

Dynamic worship is more a matter of the spirit of the people than it is the style of the service. With the right spirit any worship style—contemporary, traditional, or blended—can bring a congregation into a dynamic, genuine worship experience. In the "emerging worship" trend of today, many churches have begun to recover and incorporate ancient worship elements, such as creeds, prayers, and classic confessions of faith, into contemporary worship settings. Our church has blended liturgical, charismatic, and Pentecostal elements together. To the glory of God, a wonderful, powerful, and eclectic worship style has been birthed. Jesus says that true worshipers must worship God "in spirit and truth" (John 4:24). This means that worship must engage our whole being—body, mind, and spirit. In 1 Corinthians 14:15 Paul writes, "What is the conclusion then? I will pray with the spirit, and I will also pray with the understanding. I will sing with the spirit, and I will also sing with the understanding."

Genuine worship fosters unity in the church because it tears down barriers. It is impossible for any of us to worship God in spirit and truth and be at odds with our neighbor. Jesus said in his Sermon on the Mount, "If you bring your gift to the altar, and there remember that your brother has something against you, leave your gift there before the altar, and go your way. First be reconciled to your brother, and then come and offer your gift" (Matthew 5:23-24). While it may be easy to imitate a praise experience, it is difficult to imitate a true worship experience.

Real worship takes us "behind the veil," where we encounter God and he begins to shed light on those things in us that are contrary to his Spirit. Too often our praise becomes an "activity," while worship involves intimacy and contemplation. Any church that begins to walk in the unity fostered by dynamic worship is primed for growth.

Sound Doctrine

In addition to having a vision, keeping Christ central, preaching biblically, praying purposefully, and worshiping dynamically, growing churches are careful to establish themselves on the firm footing of sound doctrine. Simply stated, doctrine is what we believe; it is the "meat," the "solid food" of our faith; and it is derived from the teachings of the Bible. The early church in the Book of Acts "continued steadfastly in the apostles' doctrine" (Acts 2:42), which means that those believers continually exposed themselves to the teachings of the apostles, who taught not their own ideas or concepts but the truths they had received directly from Jesus himself as the Holy Spirit gave them understanding.

If we want our churches to grow, we must be clear about what we believe and why. First Peter 3:15 says, "But sanctify the Lord God in your hearts, and always be ready to give a defense to everyone who asks you a reason for the hope that is in you." Many Christians today struggle continually with willful sin and do not grow strong spiritually because they have never become grounded in the biblical teachings or doctrines of the faith. Because of this they become easy prey for the enemy and their lives display little evidence of the fruit of the Spirit.

Everyone has a worldview—a way of looking at the world and trying to understand it. Another way to define doctrine is to say that it is the "worldview" of the church that defines what we believe about God, humanity, salvation, good and evil, and the world in general. Doctrine defines what we believe the Bible teaches about all these things. This is one reason why every first

Sunday at the Cathedral we recite the Nicene Creed or the Apostles' Creed together. These statements give us in a nutshell the basic tenets of our faith. They not only help us understand what we believe but also link us to those believers of previous generations who have walked the road of faith before us. Sound doctrine is important because it helps us avoid error and deception and provides us with a historical grounding to what we know and believe.

Comprehensive Christian Education

In generations past, Christian education for most churches meant Sunday school and little else. Certainly the systematic teaching of God's Word to people of all ages should be a top priority of the church. The future of the Christian faith depends in every generation on how well the leaders in each generation teach and prepare the leaders of the next generation.

For many years teaching the Bible in church was sufficient Christian education because everyone, even the unchurched, had grown up in a Christianized culture and knew at least the basics of what Christianity was all about. This is no longer true. We can no longer assume that the people we are trying to reach have at least a modicum of knowledge about the Christian faith. Because of our postmodern culture and the increasing number of people in this country who were raised in other cultures and faith systems, more Americans than ever before are growing up with no knowledge at all of the teachings of Christianity.

At the same time, more and more of the people we hope to reach with the gospel are growing up without knowledge or training in even the most basic social skills that are necessary for success and prosperity. They cannot read or write well enough to fill out a job application. They have no clue as to how they should dress or behave for a job interview to increase their chances of being hired. They know nothing about financial planning or even how to set up a simple budget. These are only a few examples.

It is all of these areas and more, and not just Bible study, that the church today must address in meeting its responsibility to educate people in the faith and bring them to maturity. Growing churches seek to address the needs of the *whole* person, and a comprehensive program of Christian education is an important part of the process.

Holy Living

An inseparable component of all the other foundational elements for a growing church is the requirement for holy living. The Lord has called every believer without exception to a life of personal holiness. First Peter 1:15-16 says, "As He who called you is holy, you also be holy in all your conduct, because it is written, 'Be holy, for I am holy.'" Because God is holy, we cannot expect him to bless or anoint either individuals or churches that are not committed to lifestyles of personal and corporate holiness.

Holiness is the critical prerequisite to all the blessings of God. To be holy means to live in a conscious state of being set apart for God and striving to live in a manner consistent with God's Word. A holy lifestyle involves, among other things, moral purity, honor, honesty, integrity, truthfulness, trustworthiness, and good character. Paul's list of the fruit of the Spirit in Galatians 5:22-23 is also a concise description of the characteristics of holy living: "love, joy, peace, longsuffering, kindness, goodness, faithfulness, gentleness, self-control."

In practical terms, holiness in a church should be modeled by the leadership and be a standard for the congregation as a whole. More often than not, churches take on the character and priorities of their pastors and leaders, which is why pastors and leaders who want to see their churches grow must be committed personally to a lifestyle of the highest standard of moral integrity. Consistent godly living is never easy. Paul exhorted Timothy, "Take heed to yourself and to the doctrine. Continue in them, for in doing this you will save both yourself and those who hear you" (1 Timothy 4:16). If we want the people in our churches to grow in holiness, holiness must start with us.

Tithing

Growing churches are tithing churches. Churches that emphasize the principle of tithing recognize the sovereign rule of God over every dimension of life, including the material and financial. Like holy living, tithing is a key to the blessings of God. God says in Malachi 3:10:

> "Bring all the tithes into the storehouse,
> That there may be food in My house,
> And try Me now in this,"
> Says the LORD of hosts,
> "If I will not open for you the windows of heaven
> And pour out for you such blessing
> That there will not be room enough to receive it."

Although God's blessing is a promised by-product of tithing, there is much more to tithing than being blessed while financing the ministries of the church. Tithing is an act of faith and of worship. When we tithe we acknowledge God as the creator and owner of all things and as the one who alone is worthy of all our praise, love, and devotion. Tithing also expresses our trust in God as the one who cares for us and provides for all our needs.

Tithing is a bedrock principle of the economy of the kingdom of God. It helps us keep our priorities straight and our focus sharp by constantly reminding us of where our strength and provision, power and prosperity come from and to whom we are accountable for our stewardship.

Focus on People

Growing churches are concerned about people in need and involve themselves in serving those people in the name and spirit of Christ. James writes, "Pure and undefiled religion before God and the Father is this: to visit orphans and widows in their trouble, and to keep oneself unspotted from the world" (1:27). In James's day, orphans and widows represented the most destitute and needy in society, the poorest of the poor who had no status, few resources, and no one to plead their cause or to work for justice in their behalf. They were at the mercy of people's goodwill and compassion.

The poor, needy, and oppressed of the world are the objects of God's greatest care and concern. The Bible clearly demonstrates that God judges nations and societies according to the way they treat the poorest and neediest in their midst. Growing churches are made up of believers who are concerned about the things that God is concerned about, and God is concerned about people. Programs are important in churches only as far as they facilitate compassionate, loving service and ministry to people in need. This goes beyond spiritual needs, such as preaching the gospel and leading people to Christ. It encompasses practical ministry in social and economic areas as well.

God wants us to be concerned about the broken and the hungry, about people caught in the cycle of chronic poverty and unemployment, about people who have no shoes for their feet or proper clothes for their backs, about people who have fallen through the cracks of society. We are the church of the living God—Christ's hands, feet, and heart on earth. With this in mind, consider purchasing new shoes for the homeless instead of facilitating the distribution of old ones. After all, God gave you a new vision for growth; replicate this sense of newness in your giving.

Acts 2:44-45 says of the early church, "Now all who believed were together, and had all things in common, and sold their possessions and goods, and divided them among all, as anyone had need." Although we today may not be called to such a communal arrangement as this, the principle is the same. The early church grew in part because it was *people*-oriented, not program-oriented, and because the believers willingly gave sacrificially of themselves, their possessions, and their material resources to help others less fortunate than themselves. Churches today that wish to grow must act in a similar spirit.

This chapter is just a very brief overview of ten foundation stones critical for churches that wish to grow. Part Two of this book will deal with several of these in greater detail. At this time, however, we need to turn our attention to some important principles for growing churches that will help them build on this foundation.

4. principles of healthy church growth

❌ ❌ ❌ ❌ ❌ ❌

Every church needs a set of guiding principles—philosophical guidelines that shape how the church looks and acts and how it carries out its mission in the community and in the world. In recent years many churches have begun to utilize an effective tool for this purpose borrowed from the corporate world: the *mission statement*. As its name suggests, a mission statement defines a church's mission in clear and concise terms. It expresses how that particular congregation sees itself and its purpose. The mission statement in turn helps the church to determine the specific programs, ministries, emphases, and outreach events it needs to accomplish its mission.

Whether or not a church decides to adopt a formal mission statement, it still needs some way of understanding and defining its purpose as well as the principles according to which it will operate as a local body of Christ. The primary guidance in this process normally comes through the leadership and vision of the pastor. Churches characteristically reflect the priorities of the pastor, not because he or she issues decrees from on high like a petty despot or browbeats the congregation into doing things his or her way, but because of the moral and spiritual authority exercised by virtue of the pastoral office and because of his or her personal walk with God. The pastor's influence naturally filters through the rest of the congregation and influences attitudes and understanding of church purpose and function.

Another way of discerning the specific mission and purpose of a church is to be alert to what God is already doing in and around the church. Think about your own church for a moment. What kind of people has God placed in your church? What particular giftings and talents are evident among the members? This

church growth from an african american perspective

may be a clue to your church's specific mission. Who has God brought to your church recently? For example, has your church recently seen an influx of students? God may be leading your church to initiate a campus ministry. Are you seeing an increasing number of alcoholics or drug addicts coming into your church? As I said earlier, God may have equipped you for a ministry of helping substance abusers find Christ and get clean.

Three Basic *L*s for Growth

When I first came to Second Baptist Church as pastor more than twenty years ago, I had no plan or campaign for church growth in mind. The church was small and troubled. A split shortly before I arrived had reduced its membership from 300 to about 125. We didn't start out with any fancy programs or high-profile ministries. All we had was Jesus. As I searched for God's direction for ministry, I received a very simple formula. God said, "Love them, lift them, and liberate them." That was my mandate. The three beginning principles of my ministry were *love*, *lift*, and *liberate*. As I applied these principles, the church immediately began to grow.

I believe that these three principles are fundamental for any church that wants to grow, because they cut right to the heart of the gospel message. They define what the church is all about. Lost and broken people are desperate for love, and they should be able to find it in the church. As we *love* people and help them find Christ, we *lift* them from where they were into a new dimension of life and *liberate* them to become the people God always intended for them to be. In other words, we are engaged in the same process experienced by each of us who knows the Lord and is committed to church.

Love A popular song among younger Christians in the 1960s and '70s called "They'll Know We Are Christians by Our Love" expressed in contemporary terms Jesus' words to his disciples in

John 13:34-35 when he commanded them to love one another. Their love would indeed prove to the world that they were his disciples. Love is the lifeblood of our faith. It was love that brought Jesus to earth and love that put him on the cross. Jesus also said that love is the focus of the two greatest commandments: "'You shall love the LORD your God with all your heart, with all your soul, and with all your mind.' This is the first and greatest commandment. And the second is like it: 'You shall love your neighbor as yourself.' On these two commandments hang all the Law and the Prophets" (Matthew 22:37-40).

This is the kind of love we are to show as believers and children of God, both individually and corporately as a church body. In practice it translates into *passion* for God and *compassion* for people. Churches that display both of these in generous measure will grow, because people respond to genuine expressions of love.

Nothing can take the place of passion for God. It is the catalyst for everything else. Without a passionate love for God, a church becomes little more than a social club. Eventually it loses both its vision and its sense of direction. In Revelation 2:1-7 the Lord addresses the church in Ephesus. After first commending them for their good works, faithful labor, sound doctrine, and perseverance, he then says, "Nevertheless I have this against you, that you have left your first love. Remember therefore from where you have fallen; repent and do the first works, or else I will come to you and remove your lampstand from its place—unless you repent" (Revelation 2:4-5). In other words, all the other good things they were doing meant nothing if they did not love God with all their hearts.

Passion for God naturally overflows into compassion for people. The two are inseparable to the degree that compassionate love for other people is the primary biblical evidence that our love for God is genuine. John goes as far as to say, "If someone says, 'I love God,' and hates his brother, he is a liar; for he who does not love his brother whom he has seen, how can he love

God whom he has not seen?" (1 John 4:20). Compassion is love in action. Love is always active; love expressed in words only is not really love at all. James makes this very point when he writes: "What does it profit, my brethren, if someone says he has faith but does not have works? Can faith save him? If a brother or sister is naked and destitute of daily food, and one of you says to them, 'Depart in peace, be warmed and filled,' but you do not give them the things which are needed for the body, what does it profit? Thus also faith by itself, if it does not have works, is dead" (James 2:14-17). For James, "works" is the practical, outward expression of compassionate love, which he regards as the principal identifying characteristic of genuine faith. It is not enough for the church just to say all the right things and teach all the right doctrine; unless we show compassion to those around us, our faith is worthless and our witness empty. Remember Paul's words, "Though I speak with the tongues of men and of angels, but have not love, I have become sounding brass or a clanging cymbal" (1 Corinthians 13:1).

This kind of love is always costly. Compassion carries a price tag: a willingness to invest ourselves in people. Investing in other people means not just preaching and teaching but also caring, sharing, loving, and pouring vision into people. It means sacrificing our time, energy, money, resources, pride, self-interest, comfort, and convenience on their behalf. Jesus freely gave everything he had for us, including himself. As his followers, can we do any less for others?

Lift As important as it is, loving people in the name of Jesus is not enough by itself. It is only the first step in the overall redemptive ministry of the church. In our day people are starved for love, desperate to know that someone really cares about them. Most people will respond positively to a genuine expression of love if it comes with no strings attached. Unconditional love draws people in and often serves to disarm their defensiveness and cynicism so that they are open to hearing the message of Christ. Loving people, then, is the first step toward *lifting* them.

Unless we lift people from where they are to a new and higher place, our ministry is incomplete. If people who come to our church or who are under the influence of our ministry remain consistently unmoved and unchanged, something is wrong. Of course, we cannot effect spiritual change in people's lives on our own; only God can do that. But if we are not seeing lives changed through the work and ministry of our church—which is after all our reason and purpose for being—we should ask ourselves why not.

When I came to Second Baptist Church, I tried to lift the people through preaching and teaching. Knowledge is a powerful thing. One of the things that keeps people trapped in pervasive cycles of poverty, despair, hopelessness, and addiction is ignorance. Lack of knowledge holds people back more than any other single factor. Knowledge gives birth to hope because it awakens people to see that they have options. Hope lifts them as they begin to believe that their lives and circumstances can change for the better; they don't have to stay where they are. As I said in chapter 2, hope is essential for the health and survival of the human spirit. Preaching and teaching the Word of God lifts people up because as they hear and believe, hope is born in their hearts. And hope can become the catalyst for change.

A growing church that loves and lifts people is a church that preaches the biblical gospel fearlessly and without apology, prays continually with complete confidence, and holds up a high standard of personal holiness for *every* believer, not just the pastor and other leadership. In chapter 3 I mentioned briefly the opposition I encountered when I became pastor of Second Baptist Church. I came in preaching salvation in Jesus Christ, holiness, and the necessity of living a Spirit-filled, Spirit-led life, and some of the people didn't like it. But even if they did not like what I was doing, my opponents could not argue with the fact that God was moving, because their children were coming in droves to meet the Lord personally. I would show up at the elementary and high schools unannounced to talk with these young people. I would also go to crack houses with the deacons. Crack addicts and alcoholics were getting clean and sober and were coming to Christ. Prostitutes were being reborn and leaving their lives of sin. I would invade their space on the street corners with the elders to bear witness to the power of Jesus Christ. God moved, and people were lifted up out of dead-end lifestyles and circumstances into new lives of possibility and promise in Jesus Christ.

At the heart of the church's call to lift people is our passionate desire to see them come into a right relationship with God through Jesus Christ. This is in keeping with the ministry of reconciliation that God has charged to us. Just as we have been reconciled to God, we also are called to the ministry of reconciling others to him. In Paul's words:

> Therefore, if anyone is in Christ, he is a new creation; old things have passed away; behold, all things have become new. Now all things are of God, who has reconciled us to Himself through Jesus Christ, and has given us the ministry of reconciliation, that is, that God was in Christ reconciling the world to Himself, not imputing their trespasses to them, and has committed to us the word of reconciliation. Now then, we are ambassadors for Christ, as though God were pleading through us: we implore you on Christ's behalf, be reconciled to God.
> —2 Corinthians 5:17-20

All of us who know Christ already know what it is to be lifted up from where and what we were to a life of joy and blessing that we never would have imagined. All around us are countless thousands of people who are still waiting for that experience. It is our calling from God to lift them up just as we have been lifted up. Then both we and they will be able to say with the psalmist David:

I waited patiently for the LORD;
And He inclined to me,
And heard my cry.
He also brought me up out of a horrible pit,
Out of the miry clay,
And set my feet upon a rock,
And established my steps.
He has put a new song in my mouth—
Praise to our God;
Many will see it and fear,
And will trust in the LORD.
—Psalm 40:1-3

Liberate As the church loves people and lifts them up through the power and truth of the gospel, we can help them become truly liberated, perhaps for the first time in their lives. Truth liberates. Jesus said, "If you abide in My word, you are My disciples indeed. And you shall know the truth, and the truth shall make you free" (John 8:31-32). Liberation in this sense means not only setting people free from sin through faith in Christ but also freeing them to pursue their full potential, to press forward to become all that God intends for them to be.

God has a wonderful destiny planned for everybody, but many people live day in and day out completely unaware of this destiny. Poverty, addiction, ignorance, spiritual blindness, and other negative influences prevent them from realizing who they really are and the potential for greatness that resides in them. Part of the ministry of the church is to liberate people by awakening that awareness and helping them on the road to realizing their God-given destiny.

When I became pastor of the Second Baptist Church, I sought to liberate the people by preaching messages that were biblically based, doctrinally sound, and socially relevant. I preached on economic empowerment because so many of the people were trapped in self-defeating and self-destructive cycles of poverty, joblessness, and addiction. I preached on the empowerment of women at a time when it was not as popular for women to be in ministry as it is now. I preached on the role and responsibility of manhood to confront absentee fathers and the destructive behavior found in physically abusive relationships.

I also changed the liturgy and order of our worship services. Although we were a Baptist church, I introduced more liturgical elements. Of course, I retained many things, such as the invocation and the Scripture readings, but I also began to follow the liturgical calendar. I taught the church about Advent and Lent and Pentecost, and we sang hymns accordingly. I even initiated the practice of processing down the center aisle with an uplifted cross leading the way. Visual elements such as this can be very powerful, because they imprint a lasting image in the mind that helps us remember the truth represented by that image. Because of our eclectic worship style, many people outside our church often wondered just what kind of church we were. They couldn't categorize us, which is just what I intended. I continue to be amazed at how God can take formal historic high church liturgy and blend it with charismatic Pentecostal spontaneity and make it work. Yet week after week we allow the Holy Spirit full rein, and indeed he moves as he desires, and we are blessed.

For a church to grow, it cannot be boxed in—that is, it cannot be labeled or categorized. A growing church is unpredictable, not in the sense of being impulsive and disorderly, but in not always conforming to convention or traditional expectations. Paul said, "Let all things be done decently and in order" (1 Corinthians 14:40), but that doesn't necessarily mean being bland or predictable or even quiet. There are times for quiet reflection and times for boisterous celebration. There are times for tearful, contemplative worship and times for joyous laughter. Many church traditions have outlived their usefulness and result today only in tying people's hands and hearts so that they cannot worship or learn about God or experience God's power and presence as freely as they should. As a result, their spiritual growth is stunted and they never reach maturity in the faith.

The moment the church becomes predictable it becomes explainable, and people can easily write it off as insignificant. However, a church that develops a reputation as a place where the unpredictable and unexpected are commonplace—within biblical guidelines, of course—is a church that can make a difference in its community. People are not attracted by the mundane and ordinary. They are looking for something that will bring meaning and life to what often seems to them as a dreary and pointless existence. A church living and operating under the anointing and power of the Holy Spirit that loves, lifts, and liberates people is a bright light shining in a very dark place, and people are drawn naturally to the warmth of its illuminating glow.

The Five *E*s of a Healthy Church

Loving, lifting, and liberating constitute our church's business at all times. Everything a church does—every program, every ministry, every event—should be planned and carried out with these three principles clearly in mind. In more practical terms, this may be accomplished through careful attention to what we could call the five *E*s of a healthy church: *evangelize, educate, emancipate,* and *empower,* which together lead to *enlarge.* For the last twenty years these have been the stabilizing pillars of our ministry. Every church should examine its programs and ministries periodically to evaluate how well each serves one of these purposes. Any event, activity, service, program, or ministry in the church that does not clearly seek to evangelize, educate, emancipate, or empower people should either be restructured until it does or eliminated.

Each of these elements can be identified in the Jesus' Great Commission: "Go therefore and make disciples of all the nations, baptizing them in the name of the Father and of the Son and of the Holy Spirit, teaching them to observe all things that I have commanded you; and lo, I am with you always, even to the end of the age" (Matthew 28:19-20).

Evangelize ("Go therefore and make disciples of all the nations . . ."). Evangelizing is simply proclaiming the good news of salvation in Jesus Christ by any means—preaching, personal witnessing, ministering with music or drama, postcard marketing, or some other way. Some programs, ministries, and events of the church should be designed with evangelism as the *primary* purpose, although some of the other purposes may be applied at the same time. Some of the many examples from our church are the Mercy House, prison ministry, evangelism ministry, Bridge Builders, Embrace (HIV/AIDS support group), youth choir, Cathedral Steppers, Imani Liturgical Dance Ministry, and Cathedral mass choir.

Emancipate ("baptizing them in the name of the Father and of the Son and of the Holy Spirit . . ."). Baptism represents emancipation because it symbolizes a believer's death to the old life ("buried with Him through baptism into death" [Romans 6:4]) and birth into the freedom of eternal life in Christ ("raised . . . so we also should walk in newness of life" [Romans 6:4]) as well as freedom from sin and its penalty. Emancipation is a logical and natural follow-up to evangelism because as people believe the gospel and trust Christ, they are set free from sin and their old lives to start new lives in Christ. While baptism is an ordinance that symbolizes emancipation, a healthy church will also provide programs or ministries to help believers grow in their understanding of the freedom they have in Christ. Quite often this ties in with education. The Cathedral counseling center, prison family support ministry, substance abuse support ministry, and diaconate serve as examples of such programs and ministries at the Cathedral International.

Educate ("teaching them to observe all things that I have commanded you . . ."). Education lies at the heart of discipleship. A believer is simply a person who has trusted Christ for salvation;

a disciple is a well-informed (but always learning), well-trained (but always training), and disciplined believer who is totally committed to following Christ in everyday life. Aside from personal commitment, the main thing that distinguishes a disciple from a simple believer is education. The church's commission is to make disciples, and the best way to do that is through a commitment to organized, comprehensive Christian education, whether it be Sunday school, doctrinal and theological studies, or practical instruction such as job training or seminars on such things as marriage or financial planning. The Sidewalk Sunday School, teen Bible study, marriage enrichment classes, illiteracy prevention, Cathedral Bible Institute, and Joy in the City Daycare all provide powerful educational opportunities for members to grow at the Cathedral International Second Baptist Church. Education is a key step on the path to empowerment.

Empower ("and lo, I am with you always, even to the end of the age"). Empowerment begins with the knowledge of the Lord's constant presence with us and within us through the Holy Spirit. No obstacle is too big, no challenge too great for those who walk with the Lord and in whom his presence abides. Philippians 4:13 says, "I can do all things through Christ who strengthens me." Spiritual empowerment can instill the courage and confidence to press forward for empowerment in other areas of life, such as economic or financial empowerment, gender empowerment, and professional or occupational empowerment. Intercessory prayer, discipleship, wealth-building seminars, and a sound community development corporation all function as valuable pillars in our ministry.

Enlarge ("make disciples of all the nations"). It is the God-ordained nature of the church to grow, and any church that does not grow is not being true to its nature. *Enlarge* was recently added to our mission statement to empower the new building program. If we are to take church growth seriously, we need to develop marketing pamphlets that articulate vision and purpose.

At the Cathedral International such pamphlets include a vision statement—*Who We Are*; a concise plan that articulates strategy—*What We Do & Quick Facts*; a planned calendar that articulates focus—*An Overview of Yearly Events*; a listing of ministries—*Ministries and Programs*; and an introductory process for new members—*New Members*. Churches that focus on evangelism, education, emancipation, and empowerment *will* grow, although the specific manner and degree of that growth will vary from church to church.

Action Steps

1. *Take inventory of your relationship with God.* The church will not grow unless God's chosen pastor has dedicated himself or herself to a life of prayer and fasting. It is out of our prayer and fasting that the heart changes, turning from our own human desires to those of God's. Out of this turning, reconciliation between the pastor and God is secured and vision is spawned. Mini-sabbaticals, conferences, vacations, a healthy diet, and rest all assist the pastor in developing solid principles for church growth.

2. *Invest in the people you are leading.* If we are to motivate people to succeed in life, we must invest in them. Send your church leadership to the appropriate conferences. Send them to school. Spend time with them in informal settings where you can transfer to them your vision for the Lord's church.

3. *Love people for who they are.* Instead of being overly critical of what people have not accomplished, celebrate with them what the Lord has done. Create worship services that enable people to celebrate how faithful God has been in their lives. Such services create a level of expectancy for what God will choose to do next in the life of the ministry.

4. *Create internal auditing teams, ministry evaluating committees, or systematic performance evaluation processes by which the programs of the church can be evaluated and critiqued.*

Assign trustworthy leaders to the task of evaluating the effectiveness of the ministries within the church. If a particular ministry bears no fruit, the timing for it may no longer be right. Perhaps your vision needs to be remodeled or rebranded to spark the initiative of your parishioners.

Make sure that ministry leaders generate accurate reports of what has (and has not) been done. Check to ensure that those who are leading the people with you approach their assigned tasks with a prayerful spirit. Moreover, ask your parishioners if your programs work for them. To ensure fiscal responsibility, hire external auditors to confirm what has been audited internally. Report to the Internal Revenue Service on time. Make sure that the persons who audit your church are properly certified and registered with the appropriate agencies to minimize any potential for financial disaster, which could undermine the integrity of the pastor and destroy any potential for church growth.

PART TWO

✖ ✖ ✖ ✖ ✖ ✖

practical dimensions

5. purposeful prayer

✠ ✠ ✠ ✠ ✠ ✠

One day Jesus' disciples came up to him and asked, "Lord, teach us to pray" (Luke 11:1). Jesus responded by giving them a model prayer that we know as the "Lord's Prayer":

> Our Father in heaven,
> Hallowed be Your name.
> Your kingdom come.
> Your will be done
> On earth as it is in heaven.
> Give us day by day our daily bread.
> And forgive us our sins,
> For we also forgive everyone who is indebted to us.
> And do not lead us into temptation,
> But deliver us from the evil one.
> —Luke 11:2-4

Notice that the disciples didn't say, "Teach us to preach" or "Teach us to worship" or "Teach us to heal the sick." They asked Jesus to teach them to pray. Somehow these sometimes-slow-to-learn disciples discerned that prayer was the key to maintaining strong fellowship with God. They understood that effective, powerful prayer was their lifeline.

And so it is with us. Prayer is not an option or an after-thought—not, at least, for a church that wants to grow. This episode with Jesus and his disciples tells us at least two things: first, prayer is central to everything we do as Christians and, second, prayer can be taught.

Prayer is the divine birthright of every believer, which is activated the moment we act on our belief that we have a "hotline" to God.

Like everything else about our new life in Christ, however, our capacity for prayer does not come to us fully mature. We must build it and nurture it over time. The more we pray and the more we learn about prayer, the greater our prayer capacity grows. Prayer is like a muscle; the more we exercise it, the stronger we become.

At the same time, prayer is so simple that the littlest child can pray and catch God's ear. That's the wonderful thing about prayer; it is both simple and profound. The newest and most unlearned believer can pray with power while even the most seasoned disciples and most experienced prayer warriors can never exhaust the depths of the riches of God that are available through prayer.

Why then are so many Christians and so many churches disappointed and discouraged with their prayer lives? Why do so many fail to receive the answers that they seek? Why do they feel so powerless in prayer?

One reason may be that they have never learned the secret of praying with purpose. *Purposeful prayer* is a key component that all healthy growing churches share.

Purposeful Prayer Prays for the Purposes of God

Purposeful prayer means first of all praying for the purposes of God to be accomplished and for God's will to come to pass. This approach is borne out in Jesus' model prayer with the words, "Your kingdom come. Your will be done on earth as it is in heaven." Learning to pray as a church for the purposes of God to be done helps us avoid the trap of pursuing our own agendas and asking God to endorse them. Praying with God's purposes in mind means that we ask God to show us what is to be done and then get on board with that agenda. This way we can be sure of keeping our vision in focus and our priorities on track. God's purpose must be our purpose, God's will our will, God's ways our ways, God's priorities our priorities! Purposeful prayer is the way to make sure we are aligned with God in every way.

There is no way for us to know the purposes of God unless God reveals them to us. In Jeremiah 33:3 God says, "Call to Me, and I will answer you, and show you great and mighty things, which you do not know." God is so infinitely greater than we are that unless God chooses to be revealed or made known, we may never find or see God's way:

> "For My thoughts are not your thoughts,
> Nor are your ways My ways," says the LORD.
> "For as the heavens are higher than the earth,
> So are My ways higher than your ways,
> And My thoughts than your thoughts."
> —Isaiah 55:8-9

Purposeful prayer focused on God's purposes opens the door for God to come in and show us the pathways to holiness.

The more we practice praying for the purposes of God, the more astute and discerning we will become about what God is doing around us, in us, and through us. Purposeful prayer means praying in a direct manner until God redirects our purpose. For example, it is always right to pray for healing of the sick. Sometimes God chooses to heal them in this life, on this side of the grave. But sometimes God's purpose is to heal them on the other side by taking them home. Now, I am acutely aware that this is contrary to what some refer to as "word of faith" teaching! I firmly believe that our God still heals. God does heal in this life. I believe, teach, and preach that miracles are available in this life. I expect healing. I am also aware of the sovereignty of God. Whether someone is healed in this life or the next is God's ultimate decision. The more we pray, and the more sensitive we become to God's purpose, the more easily we will be able to discern when we need to shift the focus of our prayer. Quite frankly, I am challenged by knowing when to cease to pray for a miracle and to begin to prepare a soul to be returned to God, for there does come a time for a release from this life to life eternal, and discerning the voice of God at these times is essential.

Praying for the purposes of God helps us clarify our identity as children of God and positions us to be used by God as instruments of God's purpose and ambassadors of love, grace, mercy, and comfort.

Purposeful Prayer Is Specific

Mark 9:14-27 tells the story of Jesus casting a deaf and mute spirit out of a young boy after the disciples are unable to do so. Jesus has just come down from the mountain with Peter, James, and John, where he was transfigured before them. Meanwhile, the other nine disciples have experienced an embarrassing failure in their effort to cast out the demonic spirit. When Jesus appears on the scene, the boy's father begs him for help.

> Jesus said to him, "If you can believe, all things are possible to him who believes." Immediately the father of the child cried out and said with tears, "Lord, I believe; help my unbelief!" When Jesus saw that the people came running together, He rebuked the unclean spirit, saying to it: "Deaf and dumb spirit, I command you, come out of him and enter him no more!" Then the spirit cried out, convulsed him greatly, and came out of him. And he became as one dead, so that many said, "He is dead." But Jesus took him by the hand and lifted him up, and he arose. And when He had come into the house, His disciples asked Him privately, "Why could we not cast it out?" So He said to them, "This kind can come out by nothing but prayer and fasting."
> —Mark 9: 23-29

Mark makes no mention of the manner in which the disciples tried to evict the demonic spirit. Whatever they tried was unsuccessful. Jesus made it clear that this was a very particular kind of case that called for a special kind of focused prayer—prayer with fasting to help sharpen and focus the mind. We could call it purposeful prayer—prayer with a specific object in mind.

Specific prayer is always more effective than generalized prayer. For one thing, it is harder to tell whether a generalized prayer has been answered. A specific prayer looks for a specific answer, which is much easier to recognize. In addition, the Word of God encourages us to pray specifically. Jesus said:

> Ask, and it will be given to you; seek, and you will find; knock, and it will be opened to you. For everyone who asks receives, and he who seeks finds, and to him who knocks it will be opened. Or what man is there among you who, if his son asks for bread, will give him a stone? Or if he asks for a fish, will he give him a serpent? If you then, being evil, know how to give good gifts to your children, how much more will your Father who is in heaven give good things to those who ask him!
> —Matthew 7:7-11

In these verses, Jesus likens our asking, seeking, and knocking to children asking their parents for bread or fish—*specific* requests. And he goes on to assure us that God will answer in accordance with what we request! Specific requests receive specific answers.

Specific requests must be made in accordance with the will and purpose of God. Consider the words of James: "Where do wars and fights come from among you? Do they not come from your desires for pleasure that war in your members? You lust and do not have. You murder and covet and cannot obtain. You fight and war. Yet you do not have because you do not ask. You ask and do not receive, because you ask amiss, that you may spend it on your pleasures" (4:1-3). This is why it is so important for us to be in touch with the mind and heart of God both individually and corporately. James says that we pray "amiss" whenever we pray selfishly or outside the will of God. To pray amiss also means to pray without purpose—without plan, direction, or focus. Too often at the end of the day, we wonder why we cannot check off any answers to our prayers. Could it be that we received no answers from God because we have not asked God for anything with purpose?

Many believers are reluctant to pray specifically in the mistaken belief that to do so will presume upon God. On the contrary, God wants us to pray specifically so he can give specific answers. God desires us to pray boldly, with confidence and assurance, and with faith. As John the apostle assures us, "Now this is the confidence that we have in Him, that if we ask anything according to His will, He hears us. And if we know that He hears us, whatever we ask, we know that we have the petitions that we have asked of Him" (1 John 5:14-15).

Purposeful Prayer Builds Faith

Purposeful prayer builds our faith. As we learn to pray specifically and with purpose, we begin to see specific answers. These results in turn strengthen our faith and increase our confidence to pray even more boldly and specifically. In Psalm 138:3, David says, "In the day when I cried out, You answered me, and made me bold with strength in my soul." In effect David is saying, "I cried out to you, O Lord. I made my request known to you, and you answered me. Your answer was not only to inspire me to give you praise, but to develop something in me. You gave me something that struck a chord within my soul, and my soul grew strong. My faith grew strong, and you gave me a new boldness."

Faith is key to answered prayer. Once again, hear the wise counsel of James: "If any of you lacks wisdom, let him ask of God, who gives to all liberally and without reproach, and it will be given to him. But let him ask in faith, with no doubting, for he who doubts is like a wave of the sea driven and tossed by the wind. For let not that man suppose that he will receive anything from the Lord; he is a double-minded man, unstable in all his ways" (1:5-8). Answered prayer in one area instills in us the boldness, assurance, and faith to continue to pray in that area and also to expand our prayer into other areas. Answered prayer assures us that God is listening, and that is a precious assurance in an uncertain world. Answered prayer gives birth to the faith agent in even the weakest among us. By strengthening our faith, answered prayer enables us to pray with confidence in spite of what we see, even when what we see is the direct opposite of what we are praying for. "Now faith is the substance of things hoped for, the evidence of things not seen" (Hebrews 11:1). Answered prayer helps us understand that there is more to truth and reality than meets the eye.

One day Jesus and his disciples were crossing the Sea of Galilee. Jesus was asleep in the back of the boat. Suddenly a severe storm arose—a common occurrence on that body of water. High winds and heavy waves threatened to swamp the boat. Jesus' disciples were terrified. Convinced that they were about to drown, they awakened Jesus. "'Teacher, do You not care that we are perishing?' Then He arose and rebuked the wind, and said to the sea, 'Peace, be still!' And the wind ceased and there was a great calm. But He said to them, 'Why are you so fearful? How is it that you have no faith?' And they feared exceedingly, and said to one another, 'Who can this be, that even the wind and the sea obey Him!'" (Mark 4:38-41). The critical point here is Jesus' question, "How is it that you have no faith?" Lack of faith was a problem for the disciples for a long time. Even after spending three years with Jesus, they still did not understand many things. One of the reasons they were unable to cast out the deaf and mute spirit from the young boy was their lack of faith. For most of the disciples it took until the day of Pentecost to make sense of all the things they had seen and heard while they were with Jesus.

The disciples were faithful, but they were not faith-filled. God wants us to be both. Purposeful prayer can fill us with faith as we see our prayers answered. And God honors our faithfulness by moving in our lives and churches in such a way as to further increase and strengthen our faith. Hebrews 6:10 says, "For God is not unjust to forget your work and labor of love which you have shown toward His name, in that you have ministered to the saints, and do minister." God honors our faithfulness but also wants us to have faith—genuine, mountain-moving faith. This kind of faith is one of the results of purposeful prayer.

Purposeful Prayer Purifies Us

Another important value of purposeful prayer in our individual and corporate Christian lives is its purifying power. Purposeful prayer purifies us by cleansing our motives and desires and clarifying our needs. The more we learn to pray with purpose, the more we will understand the difference between the real and the false, between our needs and our wants, and between the meat and the fat in our lives. Purposeful prayer will show us where and how to target our resources so that we can be good stewards of what God has given. Too many churches waste resources maintaining programs that no longer serve a legitimate purpose or pursuing agendas other than God's. Discouragement often sets in when they fail to grow and the resources needed for critical things are strained.

Purposeful prayer purifies us also by purging from our lives and hearts selfishness, greed, ungodliness, and issues contrary to God's will and Spirit. Through consistent, purposeful prayer, the Lord will purge from us unbelief, pride, bad attitudes, fleshly desires, selfishness, fear, anger, bitterness, unforgiveness, and bondage to sin. Purposeful prayer will help us learn to walk in holiness before God.

Purging occurs when God reveals things in our lives that need to be cleaned up and we willingly say, "Do it, Lord. Put your finger on my attitude. Put your finger on my meanness. Put your finger on my temper. Put your finger on my pride. Put your finger on my jealousy. Put your finger on my greed. Put your finger on my lust." Our prayer becomes that of David:

> Purge me with hyssop, and I shall be clean;
> Wash me, and I shall be whiter than snow. . . .
>
> Create in me a clean heart, O God,
> And renew a steadfast spirit within me.
> —Psalm 51:7, 10

Once we are purged of the self-serving things that have blinded us, we will be able to see what God wants us to see and to respond accordingly: to the sick and the poor and the needy; to the broken and the destitute and the homeless; to the lost and the dying and the hopeless. The genuineness of our faith, both as individuals and as churches, will be measured by how we treat "the least of these," as Jesus taught in the following parable:

> When the Son of Man comes in His glory, and all the holy angels with Him, then He will sit on the throne of His glory. All the nations will be gathered before Him, and He will separate them one from another, as a shepherd divides his sheep from the goats. And He will set the sheep on His right hand, but the goats on the left. Then the King will say to those on His right hand, "Come, you blessed of My Father, inherit the kingdom prepared for you from the foundation of the world: for I was hungry and you gave Me food; I was thirsty and you gave Me drink; I was a stranger and you took Me in; I was naked and you clothed Me; I was sick and you visited Me; I was in prison and you came to Me." Then the righteous will answer Him, saying, "Lord, when did

we see You hungry and feed You, or thirsty and give You drink? When did we see You a stranger and take You in, or naked and clothe You? Or when did we see You sick, or in prison, and come to You?" And the King will answer and say to them, "Assuredly, I say to you, inasmuch as you did it to one of the least of these My brethren, you did it to Me."
—Matthew 25:31-40

Purposeful prayer pursues God. It goes after God's will and way. Purposeful prayer is specific. Purposeful prayer prevails until the answer comes. Purposeful prayer purges sin from our hearts, reaching things that nobody knows lie within us but God.

Action Steps

Understanding the concept of purposeful prayer is one thing; developing it and making it a vital part of your life is another. Purposeful prayer is a critical key to healthy church growth, but how can a church that desires to grow develop into a church that prays with purpose? Here are some practical ideas. The primary purpose of these steps is not to provide theory on prayer, but to get as many church people as possible actively engaged in the ministry of purposeful prayer.

1. *Preach on prayer.* Build faith in the people by keeping prayer before them all the time through periodic preaching on prayer. Perhaps offer a sermon series on great prayers of the Bible, the Lord's Prayer, or biblical guidelines for effective prayer. The possibilities are many and varied.

2. *Teach on prayer.* Purposeful prayer is an excellent subject for study in Sunday school classes. In addition, many excellent in-depth studies on prayer are available from many different sources. Provide the people of the church with the opportunity to study and learn about (and put into practice) various kinds of prayer, such as petition, supplication, and intercession. Teaching and preaching on prayer could be coordinated for even greater impact.

3. *Keep an ongoing prayer list for the church that people can refer to and add to as the need arises.* Our weekly church bulletin has a "Sick and Shut-in List" noting those among us who are ill. At designated points in the church service, the corporate body prays for the restoration of these individuals or for strength to endure their time of trial. A church should come together at regular times to pray for the specific requests on the church prayer list. Encourage all church members to maintain a personal prayer list, making their requests as specific as possible. These lists provide an excellent way to record not only prayer requests but also answers to prayer, producing an ever-growing written testimony to God's faithfulness and power in answering prayer. This alone is a great faith builder.

4. *Keep a prayer journal.* Encourage every church member to record in a prayer journal their personal daily or regular encounters with God—their prayers to God and God's responses. A prayer journal is like an expanded prayer list; in fact, the prayer list in number 3 could become the framework for a prayer journal. The main difference is that the journal affords space for personal comments, insight, and reflection.

5. *Set up a telephone or e-mail prayer chain for rapid communication of prayer needs in the church.*

6. *Establish regular weekly gatherings for prayer.* Consider having midweek prayer meetings; small group prayer meetings held at various times, such as early morning, lunchtime, or evening; and weekend prayer vigils where people gather for extended periods of focused prayer.

7. *Schedule periodic prayer retreats or prayer conferences at your church.* Provide the people with in-depth study and training, inspiration and encouragement, and opportunities for extended, concentrated, and focused prayer. Typically in the first month of every year, twenty-one days are set aside at the Cathedral for consecration. It is a time for the church to collectively engage in purposeful prayer. Not only do we suspend all activities during these twenty-one days, but we worship every night, seeking to receive what God desires to communicate to us as a church family. Here again, the purpose of prayer directly correlates with our intention to grow. The more people we challenge to engage actively in the ministry of purposeful prayer, the more the church postures itself for healthy growth.

8. *Mentor prayer.* Identify gifted and experienced "prayer warriors" in your church and assign willing "prayer apprentices" to them who, through the mentoring process, will become prayer warriors themselves.

9. *Allow time in every church gathering for people to share how God is answering prayer and working in their lives and in the lives of friends and loved ones.* Conclude with a time of praise and celebration for God's goodness and faithfulness.

6. prophetic preaching

A growing African American church is a Bible-preaching and Bible-teaching church with a balanced message between priestly and prophetic ministry. Every ministry and activity of the church centers around the proclamation of the Bible as the true and living Word of God. Although there are many ways for a church to proclaim God's Word, preaching is primary. Preaching provides the framework on which all other teaching and proclamation of the church hangs. Very often the quality of a church's preaching will determine the quality of everything else the church does. One could venture to say that as the preaching goes, so goes the church. If the preaching is good and biblically sound, the rest of the church's witness and ministry should be the same. Preaching that is unsound and unbalanced, on the other hand, will lead to a church and ministry that are out of balance.

Sound preaching to inspire church growth must be, as the title of this chapter indicates, *prophetic preaching*. In this context *prophetic* does not refer to speaking prophecies as much as it does to speaking boldly and simply the full and complete Word of God. Simply stated, prophetic preaching is true to the spirit and meaning of the biblical text while at the same time speaking relevantly and redemptively to the issues, challenges, problems, and circumstances of daily life. It is one thing to know the Word of God; it is quite another to understand how to apply that Word to the situations we face every day. Prophetic preaching addresses both dimensions.

The goal of prophetic preaching is twofold: to bring unbelievers into a saving knowledge of Jesus Christ as Lord and to develop believers into spiritually mature disciples of Christ. Success in both areas requires careful coordination between the preaching, teaching, and service/outreach ministries of the church. In other words, the themes and focus that appear in the pastor's preaching should be reinforced in the teaching, whether in Christian education programs, cell groups, or ministries of the members of the church body to one another and to the wider community.

Close coordination of this kind takes a lot of time and careful planning, but the results are well worth the effort. Churches that learn to coordinate their preaching, teaching, and service ministries in this way maintain a unified vision and work more harmoniously toward the same goals. Coordination at all levels helps prevent different people or groups in the church from working at cross-purposes with each other. It also helps the church keep a sharper focus by avoiding programs or emphases that distract from the common vision.

A coordinated approach such as this will be successful only in proportion to the soundness of the preaching. Since preaching is the linchpin to the success of any growing church, it is crucial that the pastor be in regular communion with God. A pastor has the responsibility of guiding the church according to the vision and word he or she has received from the Lord. This vision and word must remain fresh, and we maintain fresh understanding and revelation by drawing daily from the wellspring of the Word of God.

Sound and effective preaching goes well beyond a pastor's oratorical skills. While any pastor should certainly strive to make her or his sermons as intellectually stimulating, as emotionally engaging, and as passionate as possible, even more important is that the preaching reflect evidence that the pastor has spent much time in the Lord's presence. Jonathan Edwards, the great eighteenth-century pastor and preacher in Massachusetts, was so nearsighted that he wrote out all of his sermons in full and preached by holding the manuscript inches from his face and reading it word for word. This was not a very dynamic preaching style, to say the least, yet Jonathan Edwards had such a heart for God and spent so much time in God's presence that even his dry approach was so anointed by the Holy Spirit that revival fires fell whenever he preached, sparking the Great Awakening of the mid-1700s in New England.

Prophetic preaching is preaching that taps into the latent power that resides in the Word of God, power that can change lives: "For the word of God is living and powerful, and sharper than any two-edged sword, piercing even to the division of soul and spirit, and of joints and marrow, and is a discerner of the thoughts and intents of the heart" (Hebrews 4:12). It relies not on human wisdom or philosophies or ideas but on the thoughts and ways of the living God, which are infinitely higher than people's thoughts and ways.

It is this dynamic, living quality of God's Word that lies behind its ability to change lives. Because God is alive eternally, God's Word is also alive eternally and continually at work in our lives and the lives of those around us. Prophetic preaching proclaims the Scriptures, not man's opinions about the Scriptures. It proclaims the Bible as the living Word of the living God. And wherever the living Word of God is proclaimed, growth occurs, because growth takes place wherever life abides.

This is exactly what God promised concerning the Word:

> For as the rain comes down, and the snow from heaven,
> And do not return there,
> But water the earth,
> And make it bring forth and bud,
> That it may give seed to the sower
> And bread to the eater,
> So shall My word be that goes forth from My mouth;
> It shall not return to Me void,
> But it shall accomplish what I please,
> And it shall prosper in the thing for which I sent it.
> —Isaiah 55:10-11

Preaching the Word Brings Growth

Prophetic preaching puts the living Word of God continually before the people. When we allow that Word to act in our lives, it brings growth in at least three ways: through revelation, preparation, and prevention.

Revelation First, God's Word brings growth by revealing to us who we really are as children of God and coheirs with Christ of the Kingdom of God. By teaching us our true identity in the Lord, God's Word counteracts and exposes the lies of the enemy and the world that we have bought into, lies that tell us we are of no value or that we will never amount to anything. The Bible reveals that God loves us and has great plans for us: "For I know the thoughts that I think toward you, says the LORD, thoughts of peace and not of evil, to give you a future and a hope. Then you will call upon Me and go and pray to Me, and I will listen to you. And you will seek Me and find me, when you search for Me with all your heart" (Jeremiah 29:11-13). God thinks about us and wants to give us a future filled with peace and hope. This is good news that the people in our neighborhoods and communities need to hear. People today are starved for good news, and in the gospel of Jesus Christ the church has the best news in the world. When they do hear it—whether through our personal witness or through the prophetic preaching of our church—and when they understand it through the enabling of the Holy Spirit, they will respond and the church will grow.

What does it mean to be "children of God"? The apostle Peter expresses it eloquently: "You are a chosen generation, a royal priesthood, a holy nation, His own special people, that you may proclaim the praises of Him who called you out of darkness into His marvelous light; who once were not a people but are now the people of God, who had not obtained mercy but now have obtained mercy" (1 Peter 2:9-10). Adding to our identity are these words from Paul: "The Spirit Himself bears witness with our spirit that we are children of God, and if children, then heirs—heirs of God and joint heirs with Christ, if indeed we suffer with Him, that we may also be glorified together" (Romans 8:16-17).

People who know who they are and where they are going face the future with less fear and greater hope and confidence than do people who are confused about their identity. The same is true for churches. A local body of Christ that is clear about its identity, vision, and mission will grow in every area—numerically, financially and spiritually—and have a greater spiritual and prophetic impact in its community than will a church that is still trying to "find itself" or is caught in a web of irrelevant or uncoordinated programs and ministries. Prophetic preaching plays a critical role in defining this identity both for individuals and for the corporate church.

The revelatory Word of God has power; not only power for the present, but also power to speak into our future. In other words, by embracing what God's Word says about us today, we can determine and settle our future for tomorrow and forever. Our future doesn't have to be a fog of uncertainty and fear. Instead, we can face it with joy and hope, proclaiming in all confidence, "I will live for Christ! I will be consecrated! I will be set apart! I will succeed!" This is borne out by Paul's words to Timothy: "Therefore if anyone cleanses himself from the latter [the old life of sin], he will be a vessel for honor, sanctified and useful for the Master, prepared for every good work" (2 Timothy 2:21).

Preparation Second, the Word of God prepares us "for every good work." Not only does God's Word reveal to us who we are, but it also prepares us for living a holy life that is acceptable to God and is a key to spiritual growth and victory. Psalm 119, the longest psalm in the Bible, is devoted to the subject of the importance and power of the Word of God in our lives. It says in part:

How can young people keep their way pure?
   By guarding it according to your word.
With my whole heart I seek you;
   do not let me stray from your commandments.
I treasure your word in my heart,
   so that I may not sin against you.
—Psalm 119: 9-11, NRSV

Even though verse 9 refers to "young people," these verses apply equally to men and women of all ages. Regardless of our age or gender, as believers we are called to a holy life, and the only way to achieve that is by living according to God's Word. This is another reason why prophetic preaching is so important. Many "voices" in our culture are clamoring for our attention— voices that will lead us either to good or evil, health or sickness, prosperity or poverty, success or failure, life or death. Many people, even a lot of Christians, are confused about which voice to listen to. In our day more than any other, it is vital for the church to speak with a clear, uncompromising voice, to call people from their confusion into the clarity of the Word of God.

In the church, this clarity of voice must begin with the pastor. He or she must set the example in both word and deed if the rest of the church is to follow. God's Word is all we need to enlighten and enable us to live lives of personal power and purpose. Living according to God's Word will prepare us for a life pleasing to God, a life that fulfills the destiny planned for us as God's children. In the words of Paul, "All Scripture is given by inspiration of God, and is profitable for doctrine, for reproof, for correction, for instruction in righteousness, that the man [or woman] of God may be complete, thoroughly equipped for every good work" (2 Timothy 3:16-17).

To say that the Bible is inspired by God literally means that it is "God-breathed." In other words, the Bible is not a dead book of dry religious laws and rituals, but the living truth of God himself. It teaches us what to believe (doctrine), convicts us when we sin (reproof), adjusts our thinking and behavior to keep us on the right path (correction), and teaches us how to walk in holiness (instruction in righteousness) so that we may grow to maturity (be complete), totally prepared to carry out the call of God in our lives (thoroughly equipped for every good work). Because the Bible is the inspired Word of God, anyone who preaches or proclaims it can be confident that everything he or she says is absolutely true even in the midst of a culture that increasingly denies the existence of absolute truth.

Prevention Third, the Word of God actively applied in our lives serves as a preventative. When we live according to the Word of God and allow it to become personally real to us, it prevents some things that might otherwise have happened to us somewhere down the road. It protects us from or delivers us through life's storms as well as from the enemy's schemes. God has protected me from many things because I accepted Christ as a child. I am convinced that I was spared much difficulty and heartache because the blood of Jesus was applied to my life at an early age.

Ecclesiastes 12:1 says:

> Remember now your Creator in the days of your youth,
> Before the difficult days come,
> And the years draw near when you say,
> "I have no pleasure in them."

For obvious reasons it is better to come to the Lord at a young age. Nevertheless, regardless of how old we are or how much we have been through, it is never too late to allow God to apply the healing, saving, and preventative power of God's living Word to our lives and circumstances.

Prophetic preaching plays a key role in this process. Think of all the young people who, because they heeded the Word of God preached in their church, were spared a life broken by crime, addictions, out-of-wedlock pregnancies, or divorce. Of course, many, many people in our communities have already been devastated by these things. But just think of the ones who have been spared further heartache and destruction because, even later in life, they heard God's Word preached, heeded it, and got their lives cleaned up and set on a new and godly path.

Jesus said, "You shall know the truth, and the truth shall make you free" (John 8:32). God's Word is truth. Prophetic preaching proclaims God's Word; therefore, prophetic preaching can help prevent people from giving in to falsehoods and error that could destroy their lives. Deuteronomy says: "See, I have set before you today life and good, death and evil, in that I command you today to love the LORD your God, to walk in His ways, and to keep His commandments, His statutes, and His judgments, that you may live and multiply; and the LORD your God will bless you in the land which you go to possess. . . . I have set before you life and death, blessing and cursing; therefore choose life, that both you and your descendants may live" (30:15-16,19). How we respond to the Word of God is a matter of life and death, and prophetic preaching can make all the difference.

Preaching the *Whole* Bible Brings Growth

Preaching the *whole* Bible, from Genesis to Revelation, proclaiming the full and complete gospel message, is also a catalyst to church growth. Far too much of today's teaching and preaching is elementary. We have come to be preachers of a crossless gospel. The full gospel is both vertical and horizontal. It reaches heaven and humanity! The Bible as we have it in the Old and New Testaments presents a unified message and revelation of God's Person, nature, ways, and redemptive activity in the lives and affairs of humankind. The people in our churches and communities need and deserve to hear the full scope of God's written revelation. We who are pastors and preachers have a solemn and holy responsibility to preach the *whole* Word of God without being selective of the themes or the portions of Scripture we choose to emphasize.

Across the entire spectrum of the Christian church today we can find many examples of selectivity in preaching. Some churches and individuals emphasize healing or holiness while others focus on social issues. Still others major on prophecy or preach a prosperity message. While each of these is a *part* of the biblical gospel message, by themselves they are incomplete. Churches that major on these themes to the virtual exclusion of others preach an incomplete gospel, which leads to incomplete understanding and even error, resulting in believers who are spiritually, theologically, and sometimes even morally unbalanced.

In some cases, selectivity in preaching can lead to great harm. Former televangelist Jim Bakker, for example, whose popular television ministry collapsed under a cloud of financial impropriety and who served a prison term as a result, has identified selectivity in his preaching as part of the reason for his failure. He has since repented and returned to the Lord and now says that if he were to do it all over again he would not focus so exclusively on preaching prosperity. Rather, he would proclaim a more mature, balanced gospel message.

From Genesis to Revelation the Bible is the divinely inspired Word of God, and as such it speaks to all aspects of the human condition. It tells us where we came from and who we were meant to be in God's original design; it tells us how sin corrupted us and warped us into the spiritually misshapen and fallen creatures we are today; and it tells us how we can be restored to the people God intended us to be from the start. The Bible also reveals that God is the absolute Lord of all things, including human history, and that history is unfolding and will continue to unfold in a way that ultimately will fulfill God's sovereign purpose.

Any preacher who desires to see his or her church grow and be relevant to the needs and circumstances of the people in the community must be committed to presenting the *full* Word of God, applying timeless biblical truths prophetically to contemporary circumstances and realities. Of course, evangelism—preaching eternal life and forgiveness of sins through repentance and faith in Jesus Christ as Savior and Lord—must be foremost. The need for forgiveness and salvation is universal.

Beyond this, prophetic preaching that reaches people and grows churches means a willingness, under the leading of God's Spirit, to tackle even the toughest and most difficult "hot-button" issues of the day, such as out-of-wedlock pregnancies, abortion, homosexuality, AIDS, poverty, addiction, pornography, divorce, adultery, and gambling. People all around us struggle with these and other issues every day, and they need to see the light that God's Word sheds on these problems. More than that, however, they need to learn how to apply the Word of God in practical ways in their lives so they can successfully navigate through the "minefield" of these hot-button issues and come through whole and victorious on the other side.

Paul's charge to Timothy is a word that every preacher of the gospel should review regularly as a gauge for measuring our ongoing faithfulness to our divine call:

> I charge you therefore before God and the Lord Jesus Christ, who will judge the living and the dead at His appearing and His kingdom: Preach the Word! Be ready in season and out of season. Convince, rebuke, exhort, with all longsuffering and teaching. For the time will come when they will not endure sound doctrine, but according to their own desires, because they have itching ears, they will heap up for themselves teachers; and they will turn their ears away from the truth, and be turned aside to fables. But you be watchful in all things, endure afflictions, do the work of an evangelist, fulfill your ministry.
> —2 Timothy 4:1-5

Action Steps

1. *Preach according to the Christian calendar.* One way to build a balanced program of biblical preaching is to use the Christian liturgical calendar as a guideline. The calendar provides designated or suggested Scripture passages for each Sunday as well as themes for each Sunday and season of the Christian year. (Such a calendar is likely to be available through your denomination or local Christian bookstores.) Paying attention to these Scriptures and themes as well as to seasonal emphases, such as Advent, Christmas, Epiphany, Lent, Easter, and Pentecost, can provide abundant ideas for preaching topics in a way that will carry a congregation progressively and systematically through the biblical revelation as a whole. If this sounds too "mechanical" to you, remember that the Holy Spirit can and does honor planning and preparation as much as spontaneity. Furthermore, the Lord desires even more than we do that people understand and live according to the Scriptures.

2. *Keep it simple.* Generally speaking, biblical illiteracy is more prevalent in our day than perhaps at any other time in the history of our nation. Up until about a generation ago we could safely assume that the people sitting in our pews or being reached by our ministries had at least a basic concept of the Christian faith and what Christians believe. This is no longer the case. More and more Americans are growing up with little or no knowledge of the church or even the basics of the faith. Unfortunately, the same is true for many believers. Perhaps never before have there been as many biblically and doctrinally uninformed believers in our churches as there are today.

For all these reasons and more, we need to keep our preaching simple. By *simple* I don't mean light or superficial, but basic and, above all, *clear.* Prophetic preaching can be deeply biblical and challenging yet still be simple. The greatest message in the world is of little practical value if no one can understand it. As Paul said,

"In the church I would rather speak five words with my understanding, that I may teach others also, than ten thousand words in a tongue" (1 Corinthians 14:19). There is no reason to use fancy words or highly technical terminology when simpler words will do. We are after clarity, so the simpler the better.

3. *Keep it relevant.* People all around us are starved for truth. They are looking for practical answers that will give their lives meaning and help them not only survive, but thrive each day. Many of the people we come in contact with will question the relevance for today of a book written over two thousand years ago in another part of the world. We must be careful to keep our preaching relevant and up-to-date by staying in touch with the times in which we are living and by showing how the timeless truth of God's Word can apply to each person's circumstances.

4. *Stay well-grounded.* If we want to see people's lives changed and our churches grow, we need to keep ourselves and our preaching well-grounded. This means that we need to study regularly. Paul said, "Be diligent to present yourself approved to God, a worker who does not need to be ashamed, rightly dividing the word of truth" (2 Timothy 2:15). One of the first things a pastor sacrifices when time constraints become tight is his or her personal study time. We must not allow that to happen. We have a holy responsibility to bring to the people a fresh word from the Lord, and only through study and time spent in God's presence can we do that consistently.

Staying well-grounded also means making ourselves accountable to someone who can help us stay on track spiritually. Whether it is a mentor, a trusted friend, or a local pastors' fellowship, we all need an avenue through which we can dialogue, receive feedback, and make sure we are keeping our focus sharp and clear.

5. *Preach from the overflow.* Another benefit of consistent and regular study of God's Word and time spent in God's presence is an overflow of spiritual anointing on our lives that should come out in our preaching to bless those who hear it. Sermons based on theory or that lack the conviction of personal experience or identification rarely move anyone. Effective prophetic preaching is passionate and heartfelt, stemming from the overflow of the preacher's personal study and daily walk with God. There is no substitute for either.

6. *Preach with balance.* Again, the themes that appear in the pastor's preaching should be reinforced in the teaching, whether in Christian education programs, cell groups, or as incorporated into the church's ministries to one another and to the wider community. Close coordination of this kind takes a lot of time and much careful planning, but the results are well worth the effort.

7. powerful worship

※ ※ ※ ※ ※ ※

Growing churches place a high priority on dynamic corporate worship. Of course, true worship is first of all an intensely personal experience, one in which an individual has a life-changing one-on-one encounter with the living God. This is exactly what happened to Moses when he saw the burning bush. He worshiped the God who met him there, and that encounter transformed him from a stammering fugitive murderer who was herding sheep on the backside of the Sinai desert to a fearless, fiery spokesman for God and deliverer of his people, who even dared to face off against the king of Egypt. No one who experiences the genuine presence of God comes away unchanged.

As personal as worship is, it also has an undeniable corporate element. Christianity as a faith is both personal and communal, and each of these is incomplete without the other. Our individual private worship lays the foundation for the corporate worship we experience when we come together as the body of Christ. A growing church is a worshiping church, and a worshiping church is a powerful church. In fact, I contend that nothing on this earth is more powerful than a local fellowship of believers gathered in genuine corporate worship. When the people of God are in worship, we are extremely dangerous! The enemy fears nothing more than the people of God praising and worshiping God together.

God delights in our worship. Psalm 22:3 says that God inhabits the praises of his people. When we enter into worship as a corporate body, God honors us and visits us with divine presence and power. We are ushered into the realm where signs and wonders and miracles are possible. We receive a greater love for God, for those around us, and for the Word.

The Holy Spirit breathes on us the breath of God that waters and refreshes the dry places in our lives and raises us up as a living hope to a dying world and as salt and light to a tasteless and dark generation.

Perhaps among the most compelling biblical examples of the presence of God descending in power in response to the people's worship is found in 2 Chronicles in connection with the dedication of the temple in Jerusalem. King Solomon, son and successor of David, had completed construction of the temple that his father had dreamed of and prepared for before his death. On the day of dedication, the priests and Levites brought the ark of the covenant into the temple and placed it in the Most Holy Place. The king and the people were sacrificing sheep and oxen beyond number. This is what happened after the priests came out of the Most Holy Place:

> Indeed it came to pass, when the trumpeters and singers were as one, to make one sound to be heard in praising and thanking the LORD, and when they lifted up their voice with the trumpets and cymbals and instruments of music, and praised the LORD, saying:
> "For He is good,
> For His mercy endures forever,"
> that the house, the house of the LORD, was filled with a cloud, so that the priests could not continue ministering because of the cloud; for the glory of the LORD filled the house of God.
> —2 Chronicles 5:13-14

Following this, King Solomon addressed the people and offered a lengthy and heartfelt prayer of dedication to the Lord.

> When Solomon had finished praying, fire came down from heaven and consumed the burnt offering and the

sacrifices; and the glory of the LORD filled the temple. And the priests could not enter the house of the LORD, because the glory of the LORD had filled the LORD's house. When all the children of Israel saw how the fire came down, and the glory of the LORD on the temple, they bowed their faces to the ground on the pavement, and worshiped and praised the LORD, saying:
"For He is good,
For His mercy endures forever."
—2 Chronicles 7:1-3

The people of Israel were overjoyed at the completion of the temple. They freely offered up praise and worship to God, and God responded with a manifestation of his presence and glory that was so strong that no one could stay in the building. God answered Solomon's prayer and promised that if the people responded with love and obedience to his commands, they would be blessed beyond measure. God delights in a people who delight in worship.

Worship Says "I Love You" to God
Poet Elizabeth Barrett Browning wrote:

How do I love thee? Let me count the ways.
I love thee to the depth and breadth and height
My soul can reach. . . .

Although Browning was writing of human love, her words express what worship is all about. Worship is a way of saying to God, "I love you." That is why we must be careful never to allow either our private or corporate worship to become routine, humdrum, or boring. Otherwise, all of our words about loving God become nothing more than lip service. Love is much more than a feeling, more a verb than a noun. Love is something we do, something we live.

The poet said that her love extended to "the depth and breadth and height" her soul could reach. In other words, she loved with everything in her being. This is exactly the kind of love God deserves and desires from us and which we should openly and freely express in our worship. Scripture confirms this. To the ancient Jews, nothing in the Mosaic law was more important than the Shema: "Hear, O Israel: The LORD our God, the LORD is one! You shall love the LORD your God with all your heart, with all your soul, and with all your strength" (Deuteronomy 6:4-5). Jesus reiterated the importance of loving God wholeheartedly by calling this the "first and great commandment" (Matthew 22:38). Stated another way, Jesus told the Samaritan woman at Jacob's well: "But the hour is coming, and now is, when the true worshipers will worship the Father in spirit and truth; for the Father is seeking such to worship Him. God is Spirit, and those who worship Him must worship in spirit and truth" (John 4:23-24).

God seeks worshipers who will worship "in spirit and in truth." This means that we are to love and worship God with our whole being. We must engage ourselves completely in body, mind, and spirit. Worship is one way we affirm our love for God, and true love calls for total commitment. We also express our love for God by our obedience to God's will and Word.

If true worship as an act of love delights God, then lack of love for God is a serious offense, particularly for those who claim to know and love God. In Jeremiah 2 the prophet speaks a word of judgment, chastising the people because they have lost their love for God. They have become so familiar with God and with the rituals and forms of their religion that they have lost the excitement in God they once knew.

> Moreover the word of the LORD came to me, saying, "Go and cry in the hearing of Jerusalem, saying, 'Thus says the LORD:
> "I remember you,

The kindness of your youth,
The love of your betrothal,
When you went after Me in the wilderness,
In a land not sown.
Israel was holiness to the LORD,
The firstfruits of His increase.
All that devour him will offend;
Disaster will come upon them," says the LORD.'"
—Jeremiah 2: 1-3

In verse 2 God remembers "the kindness of [their] youth, the love of [their] betrothal, when [they] went after [Him] in the wilderness." God remembers, but these things are no more. The people have lost their love for God and will pay the consequences of judgment if they do not repent and return.

God had a similar message for the church in Ephesus:

> To the angel of the church of Ephesus write, "These things says He who holds the seven stars in His right hand, who walks in the midst of the seven golden lamp-stands: 'I know your works, your labor, your patience, and that you cannot bear those who are evil. And you have tested those who say they are apostles and are not, and have found them liars; and you have persevered and have patience, and have labored for My name's sake and have not become weary. Nevertheless I have this against you, that you have left your first love. Remember therefore from where you have fallen; repent and do the first works, or else I will come to you quickly and remove your lampstand from its place—unless you repent.'"
> —Revelation 2:1-5

The church in Ephesus had many things right: they worked hard for the Lord, were patient in their labor, knew and believed correct doctrine, and did not tolerate evil or false prophets. Yet all of that put together was not enough to compensate for losing their love for God. That loss was so serious that they were in danger of being destroyed as a church unless they repented.

Real worship is going after God with total love and complete sincerity of heart. Love for God is the fire that fuels genuine worship, which is very often a characteristic of a growing church. Consistent genuine worship in a church is rare because it is much easier to focus on doing the *work* of the Lord than it is to focus on worshiping the Lord of the work. That was the problem of the church in Ephesus. God is seeking a people who will worship and make God the focus of their full attention. We are called to be a working and worshiping people.

There are many reasons why churches fail to grow. Some of the factors are as simple as geography (e.g., African American families are increasingly migrating back toward the South, fleeing the major northern urban centers, and subsequently northern churches) or as complex as the particularity of a specific spiritual stronghold over an area. One important factor that determines church growth is a church's propensity to love. Do the people love God, or have they lost their first love? There is no substitute for loving God, and a church's worship is one of the barometers.

Worship Takes Us Deeper

"Praise and worship" has become a very familiar phrase in recent years. One should make a careful distinction between the two because although praise is an aspect of worship, it is not the same as worship. Neither is the music in the church the same as worship, yet this seems to be the idea that many church people have in mind. How many times have you heard someone say something like, "First we'll have the worship, and then we'll have the preaching"?

Worship is more than praise and it is more than music. Music is a powerful medium that can bring us into an attitude and posture of worship; and once we're prepared, it can serve as an eloquent means of expressing our worship. It is also thoroughly biblical. Whether your church has a choir or uses a worship band is not the real issue. Whether you sing traditional hymns and gospel songs or contemporary praise and worship songs is beside the point. Whether you use a traditional, contemporary, or blended worship style is irrelevant. If the spirit of worship is present in the people and especially in the worship leaders, your music can lead everyone in the building into the presence of God. Good worship music is a means, not an end.

The same is true with praise. Getting people whipped up into praise is easy. All it takes is the right beat, the right chord, the right words, and you're off. When everybody is singing and shouting and dancing and swaying and lifting hands, even an unbeliever can get in the "spirit" of things. For those who are in the right spirit, praise, like music, can be the catalyst that lifts them into true worship.

Any of us can praise, but only those who are in relationship with the Lord Jesus and in covenant with God can transcend from praise into authentic Christian worship. Worship takes us deeper. Praise is the place of celebration, but worship is the place of adoration. Adoration is the purest and highest form of love and should be reserved for God alone. And God delights in being adored. True worship is the exclusive domain of those who are totally in love with God. Reflect on John 4:24—"God is Spirit, and those who worship Him must worship in spirit and truth"—when contemplating this notion.

Worship Brings Conviction of Sin

Worship brings down the presence and glory of God, and when the Holy Spirit of God descends, people are convicted of sin. We begin to feel our awkwardness toward God and to see the reality and magnitude of our guilt, yet we are simultaneously caught up in the glory of God, which is why many people manifest the presence of God by bowing down.

Conviction brings us face-to-face with the knowledge that we are guilty before God, and that without God's mercy, we are not in a place of right standing before God. God's purpose in bringing conviction is always to lead us to turn to God in confession and repentance. This is what the prophet Isaiah experienced. When he came into the light of God's presence, he saw himself as he truly was and God as he truly is—and the experience changed him forever.

> In the year that King Uzziah died, I saw the Lord sitting on a throne, high and lifted up, and the train of His robe filled the temple. Above it stood seraphim; each one had six wings: with two he covered his face, with two he covered his feet, and with two he flew. And one cried to another and said:
> "Holy, holy, holy is the LORD of hosts;
> The whole earth is full of His glory!"
> And the posts of the door were shaken by the voice of him who cried out, and the house was filled with smoke. So I said:
> "Woe is me, for I am undone!
> Because I am a man of unclean lips,
> And I dwell in the midst of a people of unclean lips;
> For my eyes have seen the King,
> The LORD of hosts."
> Then one of the seraphim flew to me, having in his hand a live coal which he had taken with the tongs from the altar. And he touched my mouth with it, and said:
> "Behold, this has touched your lips;
> Your iniquity is taken away,
> And your sin purged."
> Also I heard the voice of the Lord, saying:
> "Whom shall I send,
> And who will go for Us?"

Then I said, "Here am I! Send me."
—Isaiah 6:1-8

Isaiah saw the Lord and said, "Woe is me!" Why did he say that? Because he was in the place of worship. In the presence of God, Isaiah saw the atrociousness of his own sin juxtaposed with the majesty, beauty, and glory of God, and it changed his perspective. Spontaneously, he cried out in confession, "I am a man of unclean lips, and I dwell in the midst of a people of unclean lips." The cleansing fire of God's grace and holiness took away Isaiah's sin, and he answered the Lord's call, saying, "Here am I! Send me."

We move from confession and repentance to cleansing and then to calling when we worship in response to God's holy presence. When we truly see God, it doesn't matter who we are or how spiritual or sanctified or anointed we think we are. For in God's presence we see that our righteousness is as filthy rags in the brilliance of God's light, glory, and perfection. And we say, "Woe is me," because we realize that our holiness cannot compare to God's holiness. We do not, however, say, "Woe is me" when we're praising God. It is only when we move into that deeper place of adoration that our eyes are opened to how sinful we really are, prompting us to confess as Isaiah did. But at the same time, we see the magnitude of what God did for us through the sacrifice of the Lord Jesus Christ in forgiving our sins and bringing us new life, which leads us into even deeper adoration.

Worship Brings the Fire of the Spirit

In his vision Isaiah also had an encounter with fire. A live coal from the altar touched his lips, purged his sin, and ignited a holy fire in his soul. When the Lord called for a messenger, Isaiah responded with "Here am I! Send me" and thus set the course for the rest of his life.

We need to make worship a priority so that, as with Isaiah, the Spirit of God can ignite a holy fire in our hearts. When we as individual worshipers come together as the corporate body of Christ, our individual fires feed off of each other and ignite others around us until the power and presence of God ignites us in one great spiritual fire that spreads beyond the four walls of our church to the surrounding community. The church will grow because people are drawn to a spiritual fire just as they are to a literal fire. The great eighteenth-century evangelist John Wesley said, "Catch on fire with enthusiasm, and people will come for miles to watch you burn."

Enthusiasm is contagious! Worship fills us with enthusiasm that manifests itself in a deep sense of joy and excitement. Just as a fire draws people, so joyful, excited people draw others in. The people and churches that are changing their communities for Christ are easy to spot because they are the ones with the inner fire of the Spirit that touches everyone they meet. They have seen the Lord and learned how to worship. We need the power of the Holy Spirit! Let it fall! Let it fall on me!

Worship Brings Inner Transformation

Fire changes everything it touches. Depending on what passes through it, fire either consumes and destroys or refines and purifies. Worship brings us into contact with the consuming and refining fire of God. God's fire consumes the dross, the sin, and the unholy. But it also refines our hearts, renews and purifies our minds, and molds us into the image of Christ. Thus, it is impossible for us to truly worship God without the results being manifested in some way. We are not stones; we are flesh and blood people with minds and hearts and spirits, so when we have been worshiping in God's presence, it will show! Others will see us and, as was said of Peter and John, will know that we have "been with Jesus" (Acts 4:13).

God is looking for people who are not afraid to let go and worship him. True worship means putting aside our fleshly, carnal inhibitions and letting God be God without caring who sees us. When we are serious about worship, we will not be hindered by our surroundings or by the opinions of others. When our Maker enters the room, we need to cast all our pride, pretensions, facades, and petty grievances and differences into the refining fire of his holiness and be transformed. For in genuine worship God is preeminent. God has shown up, and that's all that matters! The Sovereign is here, and we stand in awe and respect of God's majesty.

There is a longstanding tradition during presentations of George Frideric Handel's musical masterpiece *The Messiah* of the audience standing during the performance of his great "Hallelujah Chorus." This tradition stems from the time when the work was performed for the king of England who, upon hearing the "Hallelujah Chorus," stood up. Everyone else in the hall stood up as well, for no one sits in the presence of the king. And that should be our attitude when we come to worship the King of whom that chorus was written.

Worship is the church's love song to God. The more we learn to sing it in perfect harmony and purity of spirit, the more people outside will be drawn by its beauty. And the church will grow as many on the outside enter in to join in the singing. Then we can anticipate the day when, as that mighty chorus declares, "The kingdom of this world is become the kingdom of our Lord and of His Christ; and He shall reign forever and ever! Hallelujah!" (see Revelation 11:15).

Experiencing this inner transformation through worship is particularly important for those of us who lead in our churches. If we want our churches to grow through powerful, transforming worship, we must begin by looking to our own "worship quotient." We need to take caution that the work of the church does not consume us to the point where we move away from the God of the church who called us in the first place. We must become enthusiastic personal worshipers, and not just on

Sundays. We must regularly magnify God, show love for God's Word, and sing to God a new song. And we must allow ourselves to "get happy" every now and then in the kitchen, in the car, or wherever we happen to experience God's presence. We must personally feel the fire.

Action Steps

1. *Preach and teach about the nature, purpose, theology, dynamics, and methods of worship.* Many Christians today are woefully ignorant about the nature of true worship. They have rarely if ever experienced it because they have only a shallow commitment to the Lord. They need solid instruction in what worship is and why it is important.

2. *Train all church leaders to become enthusiastic personal worshipers.* This includes not only pastoral staff but also worship team leaders and members, Sunday school teachers, youth leaders and workers—anyone who has any leadership roles in the church.

3. *Encourage all church members to become enthusiastic personal worshipers.* Provide training if possible. Perhaps church leaders trained in worship (as in number 2 above) could take the lead in providing this training. At most of our church conferences, our praise and worship leaders teach workshops or seminars on the necessity of praise and worship in the life of the church. They also professionally record our worship experiences for parishioners who are "shut in" and as an outreach to nonmembers in convalescent homes.

4. *Establish a worship committee or council to evaluate the church's current worship level, practices, and methods and to make recommendations for changes or improvements.* Our elders evaluate our level of worship. In fact, we have a chief elder who leads the direction of the praise and worship ministry. If the worship and praise is not genuine, or if persons with the right heart but the wrong gifting lead in song, the worship experience will not be nearly as effective as it will be if the right persons are in the right place to do ministry. Our chief elder over music is trained to make the appropriate adjustments to ensure that praise and worship at the Cathedral remains at a high standard.

5. *Conduct congregational worship polls or surveys.* This will help obtain an accurate gauge of the church's overall worship "temperature," its level of understanding of worship, as well as people's preferences concerning worship styles, music styles, and other elements.

6. *Consider broadening the range and/or style of worship music.* For example, if you currently use traditional music such as hymns, add some contemporary Christian worship music. Experiment with a blended service, one that incorporates a wide range of musical styles.

7. *Consider starting an additional alternative worship service that is based on a different approach to worship and a different style of worship music from your primary service.* A wider range of styles will help the church appeal to a wider range of people, not in the sense of catering to the world, but in the sense of Paul's practice of becoming "all things to all [people], that I might by all means save some" (1 Corinthians 9:22). We implemented a 5:00 p.m. Sunday service to meet the needs of our growing Hispanic community in Perth Amboy. The music, preaching, teaching, and public reading of Scripture are all done in Spanish. While the theology and focus of the ministry remains Christ-centered, the worship alternative that we provide at this afternoon service offers the broader community a chance to fellowship in the Lord's house.

8. *Commit to excellence in every aspect of worship.* This applies not only to the preacher, but to every worship leader, every person who prays or reads Scripture, every vocalist, and every instrumentalist. God is the object of our worship and deserves—indeed demands—our very best. Since worship is an offering and expression of love for God and not a "performance," attitude and spirit are more important than raw talent, but that is still no excuse for poor preparation or sloppy execution. The church's worship should always be honest and open, but as much as possible it should also be first class.

After our executive minister determines how the service will be ordered for Sunday, our church administrative office prints the Sunday bulletin three days in advance. This early printing enables the appropriate elders, ministers, and deacons to prepare to read the Scripture in advance. Meetings are held each week to determine which church announcements are of the highest priority and thus should be pushed with the greatest emphasis. Our praise and worship leaders rehearse every week to ensure cohesiveness within the ministry of song. Our ministers of music are professionally trained to read and write music. They create original compositions that complement the traditional hymns. Together, our worship experience at the Cathedral remains rich, powerful, and theologically balanced.

9. *Be eclectic.* Try adding elements from different church traditions to your own worship practices. Examples include banners, a processional down the center aisle with a raised Bible and cross, and readings from the liturgical calendar. Be creative. Use multimedia presentations. Incorporate drama into the worship service. All of these elements can add a fresh perspective that can help people in the church experience worship from a different angle and make it a deeper and richer experience.

Finally, a word of caution: Don't do anything simply for the sake of doing it. Don't change anything simply for the sake of changing it. Everything we do as a part of worship should point people toward God and draw them into God's presence.

8. pertinent ministry

⊠ ⊠ ⊠ ⊠ ⊠ ⊠

How do you define or assess the ministry of a growing African American church? What sets its ministry apart from those of churches that are not growing? Again, it is important to understand that church growth cannot be measured just in terms of numbers and finances. Churches grow spiritually, in relevance, and in influence, which may or may not affect the size of the church numerically.

One indicator of healthy growth is whether a church has learned the importance of a unified approach in everything it does. All aspects of a healthy church's work, message, and ministry must be designed to coordinate with the church's clearly defined mission and vision. In earlier chapters I presented the necessity of a church having a clear vision and understanding of its purpose and mission. Where does a church's ministry fit into this picture? What standards should a growing church use to define its approach to ministry?

Jesus spelled out two fundamental ministry principles, the first before his crucifixion and the second before his ascension. The first principle, sometimes referred to as the "Great Commandment," is found in Jesus' response to the question of which commandment in the Mosaic law was the most important: "Jesus said to [the lawyer who queried him], 'You shall love the LORD your God with all your heart, with all your soul, and with all your mind.' This is the first and great commandment. And the second is like it: 'You shall love your neighbor as yourself.' On these two commandments hang all the Law and the Prophets" (Matthew 22:37-40). So the first fundamental principle of ministry is to love God with everything we are and to love our neighbors as we love ourselves.

The second ministry principle is found in the words of Jesus' "Great Commission": "Go therefore and make disciples of all the nations, baptizing them in the name of the Father and of the Son and of the Holy Spirit, teaching them to observe all things that I have commanded you; and lo, I am with you always, even to the end of the age" (Matthew 28:19-20). Mark records the same commission in a slightly different form and even relates what followed Jesus' command:

> And He said to them, "Go into all the world and preach the gospel to every creature. He who believes and is baptized will be saved; but he who does not believe will be condemned. And these signs will follow those who believe: In My name they will cast out demons; they will speak with new tongues; they will take up serpents; and if they drink anything deadly, it will by no means hurt them; they will lay hands on the sick, and they will recover."
> So then, after the Lord had spoken to them, He was received up into heaven, and sat down at the right hand of God. And they went out and preached everywhere, the Lord working with them and confirming the word through the accompanying signs.
> —Mark 16:15-20

In the Book of Acts, Luke provides still another perspective on the same theme when Jesus says to his disciples, "You shall receive power when the Holy Spirit has come upon you; and you shall be witnesses to Me in Jerusalem, and in all Judea and Samaria, and to the end of the earth" (1:8). We are to love God and love our neighbor and, motivated by that love, go into the world and make disciples. This is the secret to pertinent ministry that grows a church. While this may appear self-evident, even a "no-brainer," it is amazing how many churches start off well but get caught up in programs and campaigns that ultimately are at cross-purposes with their vision. Eventually they lose sight of these fundamental principles and end up completely off track. The growing church recognizes the self-defeating nature of irrelevant or contradictory programs and has learned to stay on task by measuring each ministry and program against the identified mission and vision of the church. Our executive pastor at the Cathedral, Dr. Bernadette Glover-Williams, refers to this as "leading and judging with a steady hand."

Drawing People to Church and to Christ

What does pertinent ministry look like in action? The best biblical example is found in the same passage from Acts 2 referred to in previous chapters:

> And with many other words he [Peter] testified and exhorted them, saying, "Be saved from this perverse generation." Then those who gladly received his word were baptized; and that day about three thousand souls were added to them. And they continued steadfastly in the apostles' doctrine and fellowship, in the breaking of bread, and in prayers. Then fear came upon every soul, and many wonders and signs were done through the apostles. Now all who believed were together, and had all things in common, and sold their possessions and goods, and divided them among all, as anyone had need.
>
> So continuing daily with one accord in the temple, and breaking bread from house to house, they ate their food with gladness and simplicity of heart, praising God and having favor with all the people. And the Lord added to the church daily those who were being saved.
>
> —Acts 2: 40-47

From this passage we can see that the ministry of the early church included preaching, teaching, prayer, fellowship, and sharing of the ordinances of baptism and the Lord's Supper. Practical social ministries to meet the needs of people in the community both inside and outside the church were also apostolic priorities. All of these were done in the name and spirit of the Lord Jesus Christ with the purpose of drawing others to him. These people were both priestly and prophetic.

People give many reasons for coming to church. Some say, "I come because I love Jesus." Others say, "I come to worship God." Some people come to church looking for a husband or a wife or a date. Some come because they have a lottery ticket in their wallet or purse and hope that the Holy Spirit will bless it so they hit the jackpot. Others come for similar but equally dubious reasons. And there are even some who admit honestly, "I don't know why I come. I just come."

Then there are those people—so many of them!—who will say, often with their actions more than their words, "I come because I need help" or "I come because of what the church can do for me" or "I come because I need God to do some things on the inside of me." For every person who walks through the church door with a need, there are a thousand others with the same need who will not come into the church. So the church must go to them.

Thus, the ministry of a growing church must maintain a balance between inward and outward reach and care. As believers, we come to church to worship, to pray, and to mature spiritually. We come to grow and be equipped as disciples so that we can go out into our neighborhoods and communities with the good news that Jesus saves and that in him there is hope for every situation. In the words of the late preacher Dr. Samuel Proctor, "All humanity can be redeemed." And whether we are inside or outside the church, we should offer a consistent "menu of elements of pertinent ministry." People should receive the same things from us whether they come into the church or we take the ministries of the church to them. We are called to be both salt and light and to love, lift, and liberate humanity in Christ's name.

Conviction The first item on our ministry "menu" is *conviction*. If we want to "serve up" meaningful ministry to people and see our church grow, we must know what we believe and live what we believe. We must be people of conviction whose lives, attitudes, and behavior are driven by our convictions. We must know the truth, believe the truth, live by the truth, and be able and ready to share the truth. This includes the knowledge of how to lead another person into the kingdom of God through repentance and faith in Christ. Every believer ought to know how to lead someone in the prayer and confession of faith in Christ as Savior and Lord.

Conviction means being absolutely convinced that Christ is the only way to salvation, as in the words of Jesus, "I am the way, the truth, and the life. No one comes to the Father except through Me" (John 14:6). It means being completely confident that the Christian faith is total truth. And because we live in an increasingly pluralistic society, we must respect all faith systems without compromising our beliefs. Conviction is being able to say with Paul, "I know whom I have believed and am persuaded that He is able to keep what I have committed to Him until that Day" (2 Timothy 1:12).

As believers we each must have an "I know so" in our spirit—a confident faith by which we believe in spite of what we see. The worst thing in the world we can do is allow our feelings to dictate our faith. We must know in whom we believe so that those who meet us will have their faith elevated because of it. Their faith, their joy, their hope, their self-esteem, their sense of life's purpose, their vision, their understanding of church in general, and their perception of each of our churches in particular should be elevated because they met us. They must know from our conviction that church is important not for itself but because of whom it represents.

Christ Conviction is one thing; the proper object of our conviction is another. People who come into contact with our churches and ministries should be able to look around and see Jesus in everything we do. Our every word, action, and attitude should point them to *Christ*. Every ministry we offer, every program we conduct, every class we teach, every dinner we serve, every "care package" we deliver, every service we render, whether inside the church or outside, should bring the recipients face-to-face with the Savior. The Cathedral's drama ministry's theme is "We act like we know Jesus!" In other words, we are called to act like we know Jesus.

As previously discussed, Jesus Christ *must* be central to everything we are and do. He is the head of the church and our very reason for being. This centrality of Christ must come out in every aspect of our Christian lives both individually and corporately.

One of the ways to help our churches grow is to be deliberate and unapologetic in our proclamation of Jesus Christ is. The church is built on Jesus. We proclaim deliverance in his name. We baptize in the name of Jesus (and of the Father and the Holy Spirit). We fellowship in the name of Jesus. We teach in the name of Jesus. We serve in the name of Jesus. We worship the name of Jesus. We magnify the name of Jesus. We are healed by the name of Jesus. There is no other name given among humanity whereby we can be saved except the name of Jesus. And his name is above every other name! A growing church with pertinent ministry understands the power of its founder and walks confidently in the assurance of that power.

Caring Pertinent ministry is *caring* ministry. If we want people to come to our church, we must convince them that we care. We are called to love one another, and our love must reach beyond the walls of our church building or the confines of our own little group. We must love all people just as Christ loves them and gave himself for them. Paul writes in Romans:

> Owe no one anything except to love one another, for he who loves another has fulfilled the law. For the commandments, "You shall not commit adultery," "You shall not murder," "You shall not steal," "You shall not bear false witness," "You shall not covet," and if there is any other commandment, are all summed up in this saying, namely, "You shall love your neighbor as yourself." Love does no harm to a neighbor; therefore love is the fulfillment of the law.
> —Romans 13:8-10

Jesus says to his disciples in Matthew 9:37-38: "The harvest truly is plentiful, but the laborers are few. Therefore pray the Lord of the harvest to send out laborers into His harvest." Our Lord has called us to be laborers in the harvest, but the church will reap the harvest only if we exhibit genuine care and concern. False love and artificial concern are easy to spot, and lost, hurt, and needy people aren't stupid. They are not after pity or condescending charity. Like anybody else, they are looking for authentic love, care, and concern. Churches that are full of caring believers draw them in, not with a "handout" mentality, but rather from a "hand up" position.

Many churches don't grow because they are not genuinely concerned about people outside their own circle. They lack compassion. They are satisfied with their own exclusive club. Regrettably, some churches have become more country club than church. Some members are content and have no genuine interest in growth at all. In many cases, the Holy Spirit lets them "have their way" and sooner or later departs, leaving them to continue in their own tightly circumscribed little world.

One of my favorite poems, written by the late Paul Laurence Dunbar, begins:

> A crust of bread and a corner to sleep in,
> A minute to smile and an hour to weep in,
> A pint of joy to a peck of trouble,
> And never a laugh but the moans come double;
> And that is life![1]

For many people, that *is* life. They wake up every morning and have bitterness for breakfast, loneliness for lunch, and depression and disaster for dinner. So when they come to our church or respond to our ministry, they are looking for more than a show. They are looking for answers. They are looking for hope. And *we* have the answers. Jesus can give them hope. A pertinent ministry of caring can change hopeless people's entire perspective on life so that with the help of Jesus they can see life differently and therefore live it differently, as Dunbar expresses in the rest of his poem:

> A crust and a corner that love makes precious,
> With a smile to warm and the tears to refresh us;
> And joy seems sweeter when cares come after,
> And a moan is the finest of foils for laughter;
> And that is life!

Genuine care and concern can make all the difference.

Content Next on our ministry menu is *content*. Any church that wants to grow must make sure it has solid content in its preaching and teaching. As Paul cautioned Timothy: "Be diligent to present yourself approved to God, a worker who does not need to be ashamed, rightly dividing the word of truth. But shun profane and idle babble, for they will increase to more ungodliness" (2 Timothy 2:15-16). People hear enough "profane and idle babble" from the world every day; the last thing they need is to come to church and hear more of the same. We need to make sure that sound biblical content is the foundation and framework for everything we do and say. It needs to permeate every program and ministry of the church: Christian education and life skills classes, children's and young adult ministries, the nursery, music and dramatic arts ministries, missions, clothing and food pantry ministries, shut-in and hospital ministries, and all others. Yes, every nook and cranny needs the oil of the Holy Spirit in it. People who come into our churches or respond to our ministries should receive a steady diet of the truth of the gospel of Jesus Christ, the only truth that will set them free.

Years ago a dear man in my church who has long since departed for heaven made a point of shaking my hand after every Sunday morning service. As I stood at the back of the sanctuary, Brother Percy would walk up, take my hand, lean over close to me, and say in his strong southern accent, "Reverend, you gave me something to 'chewer on' today." Of course he meant "chew on," but I always understood. We pastors need to do our best to understand where our people are. That's what pertinent ministry is all about. Everyone who comes into contact with any program or ministry of our church should go away with something to "chewer on." And it should be solid, nourishing food, not just milk. Milk is fine for babies, but as they grow they reach a point where milk alone no longer meets their nutritional and health needs. They need to add solid food. The same is true of the people in and out of the church. Healthy growth requires more than just the "milk" of the elementary principles of faith; it requires a balanced diet of mature teaching. As the writer of Hebrews says: "For though by this time you ought to be teachers, you need someone to teach you again the first principles of the oracles of God; and you have come to need milk and not solid food. For everyone who partakes only of milk is unskilled in the word of righteousness, for he is a babe. But solid food belongs to those who are of full age, that is, those who by reason of use have their senses exercised to discern both good and evil" (5:12-14). Whenever people come to church or take part in a ministry, they need to receive something they can take home and use to improve their lives and strengthen their families.

Connection Another aspect of pertinent ministry in a growing church is *connection* with those both inside and outside the church. As church people and believers, we must have solid ongoing connections with one another and with nonbelieving family, friends, and colleagues. The outside connection is particularly important if we want the church to grow. Studies have shown that the longer we are Christians who are active in church, the fewer non-Christian friends, contacts, and associations we have. This is good for purposes of dying to the "flesh" and our old sinful way of life. It is not so good when we have fewer and fewer personal contacts with unbelievers who need to hear about Jesus from us.

We must be deliberate about developing and maintaining connection so that when new people come in they will immediately find a place to "plug in." People need to feel connected or they won't stay. They need to feel useful; they need to feel that they have a part to play, something of value to contribute. For this reason it is important for the church to have a well-organized network to help people find their "niche," whether it is singing in the choir, serving as an usher, teaching a children's class, doing hospital visitation, or preparing the church bulletin.

This is not always as easy as it may sound. Before many churches can grow, they have to deal with "entrenchment" issues: "Mrs. Smith has taught the first-grade class for thirty years, and she's not about to let some upstart come in and upset the apple cart!" Church leadership must work diligently to create an atmosphere of welcome and warmth so that new people who come in will immediately sense "I'm home" and get involved. For instance, I make sure that either I or clergy from my pastoral staff meet new members on a monthly basis. Our church designed a special, monthly "light dinner" for new members to show them we want to celebrate what God is doing in their lives. When new members enter into our fellowship, they are immediately embraced by our elders, ministers, and deacons. They are led to a reception area for private counseling and then transitioned into our discipleship ministry. Eventually they are assigned to the appropriate new members' class where they prepare for ministry. This entire process is undergirded with love.

Compassion Pertinent ministry is *compassionate* ministry. Many churches today are heavy on righteous zeal and light on compassion. It is much easier to judge and condemn someone for his or her sin than to look beyond the sin to see the flawed, frightened, hurting, needy person beneath. Righteous zeal allows us to pontificate from our ivory towers without ever letting the dirt of sinful humanity touch us. Compassion is messy, sometimes even down-in-the-mud dirty as we love the unlovable and touch the untouchable. It entails risk.

I offer a word of caution here. Too many visionary leaders want more for the people than the people want for themselves. There will be times when pastors will see with conviction what God is trying to bring to pass in the life of a parishioner. For whatever the reason, the parishioner may seem to reject God's purpose for his or her life in favor of an alternative path. In these instances, I encourage pastors to remain patient and compassionate. Pray. Wait for the Lord to reveal to you what may be hindering the individual from experiencing a breakthrough in his or her life. If we are not careful, we can burn out or become depressed for a lack of breakthrough in the lives of our parishioners. Remain compassionate in your disposition. In God's time things *will* change.

If we are serious about developing pertinent ministry and seeing our churches grow, we must be compassionate people.

Compassion sets no parameters on who receives love, care, and help. The compassionate church will welcome and gladly receive all those whom God sends. Jesus always responded with compassion to the hurting and needy. We must be willing to do the same even though it means getting our hands dirty and taking some risks.

We must be compassionate toward people who are sick and toward those who have AIDS. We must show compassion to the prostitute, the drug dealer, the junkie, and the alcoholic, as well as to the prosperous businessperson who is addicted to success or pornography. We must show compassion to the married lawyer who is having an affair with his secretary and to the housewife and mother who is in the throes of a nasty divorce. All of these have one thing in common: the issues of real life. Understand this: the church must be explicit in upholding the moral standards and behavior that the Bible teaches us. Compassion does not mean that we approve of or ignore people's behavior. But even admonishing can be done with a spirit of compassion, rooted in our striving to love our neighbors as ourselves. There are hurting people among us, and they need the comfort of a compassionate Savior. We can help them find him because we are his hands and feet and eyes and arms on earth. When we share the compassion of Jesus with others, they come into contact with him through us, and he can change their lives.

Communication Pertinent ministry and healthy church growth call for establishing and maintaining clear lines of *communication*. This is important to ensure that every person, program, and ministry keeps in step with the mission and vision of the church. Pastors, staff, and ministry leaders all need to be on the same page. Imagine the bedlam that would result from an orchestra trying to perform a symphony with each instrument playing from a different page of the score! The confusion will be even worse for a church that does not practice good communication.

Ministries and people in that church will quickly find themselves working at cross-purposes with one another.

Paul asked the Corinthians, "For if the trumpet makes an uncertain sound, who will prepare for battle?" (1 Corinthians 14:8). His point was that the church needs to communicate clearly so that anyone can understand, even someone coming in from outside who has no knowledge of the church or the gospel. If we are trying to reach unbelieving people with the good news of Jesus but they don't understand what we are saying, what good are we doing? We must communicate our message clearly so that they will know who we are, what we believe, what we stand for, and whom we serve.

Character Churches that grow and minister effectively will display the highest standards of integrity and moral and ethical *character*. The character of any church will be only as strong as the character of the individual believers who make up its membership. Simply stated, character is how we live when nobody is looking. Churches grow when people sense sincerity in the pulpit and the pew. Are we true to our word? Are we true to the Word of God? Do we live according to our convictions? Do we keep our promises? Are we responsible and accountable with our money? Do we live during the week the faith we profess on Sunday? Do we follow through on our commitments? Are we open and honest in all our dealings? Do we pay our bills on time? Can we be trusted to keep a confidence? These are signs of character. While persons' gifts may help them to find their place of ministry, it is their character that keeps them growing and promotes them to the next level. At the Cathedral International, we try very hard to look at character and not just gifting.

One reason to emphasize character is that people need to feel safe when they come to our churches or when they entrust themselves or their children to our programs and activities. At the Cathedral, those who work with children and youth (as well as the volunteer teams that support these individuals) must first go through an extensive background check, including fingerprinting, to make sure there is nothing in their background that would place any of our children or youth at risk.

Character, of course, goes far beyond passing a background check. In many segments of society, an emphasis on character is rapidly disappearing. That cannot happen in the church. Character—individual and corporate—will be reflected in our ministry. Let's make sure that our character—and our ministry—are worthy of people's trust.

Consistency Closely related to character is *consistency*. If we expect to draw people into our church, they need to know that we are dependable. They need to know that we are timely and punctual. They need to know that we will follow through with scheduled programs and activities, that we won't change course or cancel at the last minute unless it is absolutely unavoidable. A current Web site or a phone tree can be helpful in communicating ministry information. Things do come up, and the people need to be informed.

Inconsistency will undermine our credibility or that of our church faster than almost anything else. People will interpret it as a sign that we don't care about them. They will think that we don't want them or that we are not really serious about our ministry. If they decide that they cannot depend on us, they will go somewhere else—or give up on the church altogether.

A growing church seeks to exhibit consistency in preaching, teaching, doctrine, character, attitude, behavior—indeed, in all things. Consistency will show people that they can take us at our word. Jesus said, "Let your 'Yes' be 'Yes,' and your 'No,' 'No.' For whatever is more than these is from the evil one" (Matthew 5:37). Our word should be our bond. If we are consistent, people will know that we mean what we say.

Class The final item on our ministry menu is *class*. Everything we do in service, teaching, ministry, and every other area should be a first-class operation all the way. Growing churches with pertinent ministries are committed to the highest standards of excellence in every area. This does not necessarily mean going to extravagant expense to acquire the absolute best of everything; that would be poor stewardship. It does, however, mean getting the best we can afford and then finding creative ways to use it to the greatest advantage.

Striving for excellence also does not mean that only the supertalented or supergifted need apply. It does, however, mean recognizing that we are children of the King of kings and Lord of lords and that he deserves—and demands—our very best. God is not honored by poor preparation, sloppy execution, or shoddy workmanship. We don't have to *be* the very best at what we do as long as we *give* our very best. Excellence is consistently performing our best with what we have. And what we have as children of God is nothing short of infinite, because what we give to God in faith, love, and obedience, he will return to us multiplied far beyond anything we can imagine. We serve a first-class, five-star God; let's be committed to serving up first-class, five-star ministry. Sadly, I have seen many church workers give secular jobs more attention than they do their ministries. They would never just walk off the job at Chase Manhattan Bank or IBM. Why should the church be any different?

Action Steps

1. *Take inventory of your church's current ministries and programs.* Identify any that may have outlived their usefulness, perhaps due to demographic changes in the church or community or to other factors. Make plans to discontinue or phase out these programs as soon as possible. Conserve your human and material resources for more relevant endeavors.

2. *When you receive first-, second-, or third-time Sunday visitors in your church, write a personal letter thanking them for attending service with you.* Sometimes a handwritten note to a guest speaks volumes on the personal touch of the ministry, especially in megachurches.

3. *Make sure that those who are responsible for transitioning new members into the church remain in contact with such persons via telephone or e-mail.*

4. *Take stock of the ministry needs in your church and community that, as far as you know, are not being met by anyone.* Which of these needs could be addressed in a practical and realistic way by your church? What resources of gifts, talents, skills, and experience reside in the people of your church that could become the core of an effective new ministry in these areas? For instance, if you live in an urban community that offers few or no banking opportunities for your parishioners, consider creating your own credit union. Charter your own school for the youth in the community. Develop your own community development corporation to rebuild where you live. Create your own travel agency. Build your own fitness center with your own health instructors. Spearhead your own health clinics. Implement your own transition housing for those coming out of the penal system. Fill your pantry with food for the homeless, the kind of food that *you* would eat. Acquire ridged reading Bibles for the blind. Build a concierge ministry for the elderly in the community. While I acknowledge that these are what you might call "out-of-the-box" paradigm shifts, these kinds of services are desperately needed in our communities. Most churches cannot do all of the above, but they can begin by doing something. Start small but think big.

5. *Increase the sensitivity and awareness of the people in your church to ministry needs and opportunities around them.* You can do this through preaching and teaching and by encouraging them to volunteer at local ministry outlets, such as soup kitchens, food pantries, clothing banks, and other places of service. Those who take up the challenge may become the core of your leadership in new and similar ministries in your own church.

6. *Before undertaking any new ministry or program, take the time and effort to provide proper training for leaders and workers.* Do not skip this step! Enthusiasm is great, but it does not equip anyone for the down-to-earth, nitty-gritty realities of modern ministry. The quickest way to kill enthusiasm (and lose workers) is by putting someone in a ministry setting who is not prepared for it. Train!

7. *Every new ministry or program (as well as all current ones) should undergo an ongoing cycle of thorough planning, careful execution, and honest evaluation with the focus on continual improvement.*

8. *Look for ministry opportunities and needs beyond the traditional "spiritual" programs.* Many people today need help in such areas as basic literacy skills, computer literacy, job interviewing, job training, parenting, and more. Be creative and open to nontraditional ministry opportunities.

9. *Plan weekly sessions with your pastoral or administrative staff to ensure that everyone understands the vision of the church.* Develop themes for them that are easy to remember.

10. *Schedule teleconference calls with your ministry heads and those who follow their lead to ensure that the laity is being properly informed of your agenda for the church calendar year.*

9. practical christian education

✖ ✖ ✖ ✖ ✖ ✖

Whenever the subject of Christian education comes up, most Christians think immediately—and often exclusively—of Sunday school. This is perfectly normal because Sunday school has been a mainstay of church life in America since the late nineteenth century, particularly in evangelical churches. Although the perceived importance of Sunday school has ebbed and flowed over the years, it still remains at the forefront of the Christian education ministries of most Bible-believing and Bible-teaching churches, and rightfully so. The Great Commission says that we are to "make disciples." A disciple is a student, a learner. Part of the process of making disciples, then, involves education. Therefore, educating Christian disciples is one of the primary responsibilities of the church.

Someone has said that Christianity is never more than one generation from extinction. As Christian parents and leaders, we have a sober and holy obligation to educate our children and grandchildren in the beliefs, ways, and practices of our faith— to pass on to them the sacred and divine truths of the gospel of Jesus Christ so that they will be prepared to take up the torch from our hands and be the light of the world for their generation. The question we must keep before us is, "If we fail in this task, what will become of future generations?" And beyond that, what will become of the world that needs so desperately to see the light of Christ?

Any church that is serious about growth will be serious about Christian education. A well-conceived, well-organized and well-run program of Christian education will promote multiplicative growth. As we make disciples and bring them into the church, we train them through education to go out and make more disciples, who are then trained to make still more disciples. And thus the cycle continues and the church grows.

The Word of God places great importance on education, particularly in the spiritual and moral dimensions of life. Teaching the next generation was considered so important to the ancient Hebrews that it was tied closely to the central proclamation of the Jewish law and faith:

> Hear, O Israel: The LORD our God, the LORD is one! You shall love the LORD your God with all your heart, with all your soul, and with all your strength. And these words which I command you today shall be in your heart. *You shall teach them diligently to your children*, and shall talk of them when you sit in your house, when you walk by the way, when you lie down, and when you rise up. . . .
>
> When your son asks you in time to come, saying, "What is the meaning of the testimonies, the statutes, and the judgments which the LORD our God has commanded you?" then you shall say to your son: "We were slaves of Pharaoh in Egypt, and the LORD brought us out of Egypt with a mighty hand . . . And the LORD commanded us to observe all these statutes, to fear the LORD our God, for our good always, that He might preserve us alive, as it is this day."
> —Deuteronomy 6:4-7, 20-21, 24 (emphasis added)

Teaching is a major theme throughout the Bible. The Book of Deuteronomy is filled with commands to the people of God to teach his ways and his mighty works to their children. Proverbs 22:6 says, "Train up a child in the way he should go, and when he is old he will not depart from it." Jesus devoted his public ministry primarily to teaching, revealing God through his words and example. In fact, the four Gospels indicate that as the day of

Jesus' death drew nearer, he devoted more and more time to training his disciples to carry on after he was gone. He even promised to send them the Holy Spirit as a permanent resident in their hearts, saying, "He will teach you all things, and bring to your remembrance all things that I said to you" (John 14:26). Paul instructed Timothy to be faithful in teaching the truths of the gospel to those in his charge: "The things that you have heard from me among many witnesses, commit these to faithful men who will be able to teach others also" (2 Timothy 2:2). He further stressed to Timothy the importance of ongoing personal education: "Be diligent [study] to present yourself approved to God, a worker who does not need to be ashamed, rightly dividing the word of truth" (v. 15).

Next to preaching the gospel for the purpose of bringing lost people to Christ, nothing the church does is more important than educating believers to become mature, confident, and committed disciples of Christ who are equipped and motivated to change their world and claim their families, friends, workplaces, and communities for God.

Christian Education Begins—and Ends— with the Bible

Where does the job of Christian education begin? *Christian education begins—and ends—with the Bible.* By this I do not mean that teaching the Bible is the only interest or concern of Christian education. At one time that may have been true, but not anymore. When I say that Christian education begins with the Bible, I mean that teaching Scripture is the first and highest priority of any Christian education program. People of all ages—children, young people, and adults—need to know and understand the Scriptures. They need to know what God says in his Word and how his Word applies to them in day-to-day life. This is the purpose of Sunday school, weekly small group Bible studies, and any other church-sponsored study with the Bible as its main subject.

Christian education also *ends* with the Bible. By this I mean that everything the church teaches must conform to and be measured by the teachings of God's Word, even if the subject of the study is not the Bible per se. For example, suppose a church offers a class on personal and family financial management principles. Because this study involves teaching, it falls under the oversight of the Christian education ministry. Everything in the study should be based on biblical principles and not simply borrowed from the world. The Bible has much to say about money and its management, and any church-sponsored study of financial management should be built on and strongly reflect biblical principles regarding money. In other words, even though the class is not a Bible study, it nevertheless should be infused with biblical truth throughout. While this may seem self-evident to many, it is amazing how many churches today borrow ideas, principles, and techniques from the world concerning "nonbiblical" subjects and incorporate them without ever bothering to evaluate them to see if they measure up to the plumb line of God's Word.

The Word of God must be the foundation and the backbone of any healthy and effective program of Christian education. It must permeate every class and every course of study regardless of the subject. In today's world it is no longer enough for Christian people simply to know the Bible; they must also be taught to *think biblically* at all times—to apply a biblical and godly perspective to every aspect of life, no matter how mundane or seemingly far-removed from "religious" activity or spiritual pursuits.

Certainly the Bible does not speak specifically and directly to *every* situation or circumstance we encounter in modern life, but it does reveal universal principles of belief, thought, and behavior that can be applied to every situation or circumstance. Take smoking for example. The Bible does not address smoking because, as far as we know, the practice did not exist in that ancient time. How then could one arrive at a "Christian" or "biblical" perspective on smoking? One way is by applying a biblical principle regarding a related issue. We know from medical and scientific studies that smoking is harmful to our health, contributing to cancer, emphysema, heart disease, and many other maladies. We also know from Scripture that our bodies are temples of the Holy Spirit and that we should take care of them out of honor and respect for God. One way to care for the body is to eliminate or avoid consuming anything that will harm it, such as smoking of any kind. A biblical case against smoking can be made on these grounds.

This is just one very simple example of how to use the Word of God to inform and shape every area of life. Many of the people in our churches today don't know how to apply the teachings of the Bible effectively in their lives. Teaching them how to do so is part of the mission of Christian education.

Implement an Integrated Program

Growing churches recognize that Christian education is not just an add-on ministry but a vital lifeline that must be tightly integrated with the overall mission and vision of the church. I have already stressed the importance of coordinating the preaching and teaching in the church to ensure a unified message and to avoid programs and ministries from operating at cross-purposes with each other. Any effective Christian education program will be intimately connected with the identified mission of the church. To illustrate how this can be done, let me use as an example the Christian education program we have in place at the Cathedral International.

The overall objective of the Cathedral's Christian education programming is to equip believers for lifelong learning in their journey of faith. We believe that effective Christian education consists of developing, planning, and implementing vibrant, comprehensive educational programming for children, youth, and adults. The mission of the Cathedral International's Christian education department directly reflects our corporate mission: "To *evangelize*, *educate*, *emancipate* and *empower* in the name of our Lord and Savior Jesus Christ through *loving, lifting* and *liberating* humanity."

We *evangelize* our community through such program initiatives as the Cathedral Summer L.I.G.H.T. Day Camp Program, the Cathedral Community L.I.G.H.T. After-School Program, and vacation Bible school.

Summer L.I.G.H.T. (Learning In God's House Together) is a day camp program for children between the ages of five and thirteen that runs for eight weeks each summer. The goal of this program is to provide a faith-based, structured, nurturing summer camp program for the children of working parents in our community. We especially target families who receive Aid to Families with Dependent Children. Summer L.I.G.H.T. spotlights the life of Jesus through such activities as Bible study, games, storytelling, and off-site adventures. We also include academic labs in math, science, and reading; athletic clinics in tennis, golf, and basketball; and an arts academy that features language arts, dance, pottery, and crafts.

The Cathedral Community L.I.G.H.T. After-School Program is designed to provide structured learning and activities for "latchkey" children of working parents who, without such a program, would be home alone for several hours after school or perhaps out on the streets getting into trouble.

Vacation Bible school is a one-week summer program designed for ages two through adult that includes worship and age-appropriate Bible study, crafts, and other Bible-oriented activities.

At the Cathedral International we *educate* believers in biblical study through our Cathedral Bible Institute's Diploma of Theological Studies program. This formal and intensive program of study, operated in partnership with Oral Roberts University School of Lifelong Education, is designed to prepare new generations of fully-equipped believers to do the work of the ministry effectively. Students in this program experience the rich history of the church integrated with in-depth biblical and theological studies. The goal of the program is to produce mature believers who are equipped to serve Jesus Christ in ministry that is marked by faith, integrity, competence, and scholarship.

We *emancipate* believers in their practical everyday living experience through Sunday morning Christian education/Sunday school class offerings. Sunday School at Cathedral International is a year-round, fully-graded, curriculum-based Bible study program for all ages. Concurrent with Sunday school, we offer "practical living" classes on such topics as prayer, evangelism, how to study the Bible, premarital counseling cycles, wealth building, financial management, conflict resolution, prayer intercession, and divine healing. There are also classes available to address responsible eating habits and weight management.

Finally, we *empower* believers by discipling them through the process of finding their place in ministry. For this purpose we established the Kingdom Citizens Institute. Formerly our new members class, KCI assists members in identifying their God-given gifts and plugging into an appropriate ministry within the church. New members classes teach believers how to be good church members. Kingdom Citizens Institute takes members to another level by teaching them how to live their lives in service to God's kingdom. Topics of study in this program include the history and structure of the Cathedral International, our doctrinal beliefs, and basic instruction in the ordinances of the church, worship, stewardship, prayer, Bible study methods, catching the church's vision, building Christian relationships, identifying spiritual gifts, and finding one's place in ministry.

Go Beyond Bible Study

Although the Bible is the foundation and framework for all Christian education, the educational focus in our churches must include more than just Bible study. As I have noted, cultural and societal changes over the last several decades have made it so that the church can no longer afford to assume that the people who come through its doors or under the influence of its ministry have any basic understanding of the Bible, the church, or the Christian faith. We can no longer assume that they have been taught even the basics of social customs and graces necessary to succeed in a career or in society in general.

In my own experience I have discovered that the church today, in order to be relevant and to truly meet the needs of people, must teach everything on every level. Christian education is Bible study, but it is also teaching about stewardship and prayer, about sexual morality and dating, and about marriage, family, and divorce.

Christian education is teaching about financial planning and wise money management, about why a person shouldn't spend two hundred dollars on an "authentic" NFL jersey when he can't afford to pay his rent, and about why a person shouldn't buy a new car when she can't afford to move out of her dingy, run-down apartment to something better.

Christian education is teaching young people (and others) how to dress for and present themselves at job interviews. It is about teaching basic manners and etiquette and social graces, getting rid of "trash talk," and speaking with intelligence and grace. Christian education is teaching people to stop seeing themselves as losers, failures, and "no-goods" and to start seeing themselves as precious individuals created in God's image.

While some of these things may at first glance seem far afield from the concerns of Christian education, remember that the object of the gospel of Christ and the mission of the church is to minister to the *whole* person; it is evangelism plus education plus emancipation plus empowerment. Many people in and around our churches are growing up (or have grown up) with little or no training at home or anywhere else in even these very basic areas, and they therefore lack the most basic and essential skills and knowledge necessary to succeed in life. Without them they are trapped in a dismal cycle of dead-end jobs, poverty, frustration, and failure.

As responsible, concerned, and compassionate citizens of the kingdom of God, we in the church who believe in and follow Christ cannot in good conscience ignore these needs. That is why Christian education today must be more than just Bible study. What practical good does it do to teach men and women the Bible when they cannot feed their own families because they lack the skills or education to get a better job? The answer for the church is not to choose one over the other but to seek to do *both*. Teach them the Bible, yes, but teach them also the biblical principles regarding honest labor. Teach them new job skills or help them find the necessary training. Teach them the importance of family priorities and self-sacrifice. Teach them what it *really* means to be human. For example, being a man doesn't mean swaggering and talking tough and throwing punches. Rather, it means honoring one's wife and loving one's kids, and striving to make a better life for them.

Like the Christian faith itself, Christian education speaks to the full scope of human life and experience. The Word of God's truth, "rightly divided," can inform, enlighten, and empower us and the people to whom we minister even when we are engaged in educational areas other than just Bible study.

Touch People Where They Are

Churches that want to grow must give especially careful attention to their educational ministry, because in our day it is more difficult and challenging than ever to get people tied into Christian education. Not too many years ago, parents came to Sunday school and brought their children. Then they began to bring their children but not stay themselves. Nowadays, many parents don't even bother to bring their children. The growing church must be prepared to find unique and innovative ways to draw people into a Christian educational environment. Some churches have started having "Saturday school" as an alternative to Sunday morning classes. We must be willing to be cutting edge and devise a ministry that works.

One good way for a church to connect with the community and mount an effective Christian education ministry is to analyze practical needs in the community and then offer training, instruction, and encouragement in those areas. People today respond to felt needs. If we offer something that touches them where they are—parenting skills, stress management, or financial management, for example—they will be much more likely to respond than they would to a general invitation to Bible study classes.

Christian education is critical for the growth of individuals in Christ, but it also helps the church to grow in number when people see the church offering assistance and training in areas that are immediately relevant to their daily lives. As long as they believe there is something that will benefit them, they will come. In some cases, assistance may be available through government or other sources, but the tremendous advantage of church-based programs and education is the infusion of the Word and the Spirit of God that imparts life and godly wisdom to people as they receive practical instruction.

Because our society has produced a generation of people who were never properly parented, the church must make up the lack and become as it were a divine parent to this generation. This is why Christian education is more important than ever and why a comprehensive and relevant program of Christian education will be a mainstay of any growing church.

Action Steps

1. *Evaluate your current educational program.* Is it exclusively or almost exclusively a Bible study-based program? If so, are there practical needs in the church and/or community that are going unmet that could be addressed by expanding the program to include Bible-based practical living classes?

2. *Survey the talent and gifts among your church members.* Are there people in the congregation already who possess the necessary knowledge, skills, or expertise to provide instruction in these areas? For example, a banker or accountant could lead a financial management seminar or an attorney could lead a clinic on wills and estate planning. A nutritionist or other health professional could teach basic diet and nutritional guidelines for optimal health. What human assets do you have already in place?

3. *Provide periodic and ongoing training for all leaders and teachers in the Christian education program so that they can continue to improve in knowledge and skills.* Our church invests in its Christian education leaders. Our pastor of Christian education attends a minimum of two conferences each year to enhance her capacity to develop new methodologies for instituting effective teaching curricula. Our lay leaders who serve in the Christian education ministry attend quarterly seminars, led by our pastoral staff, to sharpen their knowledge and skills in order to become better teachers.

4. *Evaluate regularly to make sure that all Christian education programs and classes line up with Scripture, the church's vision and mission, and the church's established policies and procedures for those programs.*

5. *Make sure the Christian education ministry secures space in which sound instruction can be provided.* Avoid moving your classrooms from one space to another during the semester. To do so only confuses the people and disrupts the continuity of exchange between the teacher and student.

10. growing a church through multiplication

⊠ ⊠ ⊠ ⊠ ⊠ ⊠

Churches grow in different ways. Some, as I noted in chapter 1, grow to become megachurches with thousands of members. This is fine if it is the proper destiny and vision for that church. Many of these megachurches, like the Cathedral International, grow by multiplication—by establishing in other locations satellite churches that are extensions of the mother church and, sometimes, by planting churches that grow and become independent.

You will recall also from chapter 1 that megachurches are and likely will remain the minority. By far the majority of local church fellowships will never attain megachurch size, nor do they need to. But this does not mean these churches cannot multiply in the same way. It is not necessary to be a megachurch to multiply either by satellite extension or by planting a new church. Midsize and even smaller churches can grow through multiplication. The determining factors are the nature of their vision and the drive and leadership of the pastor and other ministerial staff.

Handled correctly, growth by multiplication is a healthy way to grow both the local church and the Kingdom of God. Two precautions are in order, however. First, any church, regardless of size, that desires to grow through multiplication must be financially stable. Whether the new church is to be a satellite or an independent church plant, the core of the new congregation will most likely be drawn from active members of the sponsoring or mother church, at least in the beginning. The mother church must be financially stable enough to weather the departure of these people, and it must be willing to sow their talents and tithes to the new work, as well as be capable of supporting the new work financially until it is up and running on its own.

Second, the mother church must be free of internal strife and division. Otherwise, disgruntled members may transfer to the new work, carrying their dissatisfaction with them. In that case, what was intended to be healthy growth by multiplication will become instead an unhealthy and acrimonious church split. This will damage the morale, spiritual health, and public witness of both congregations.

Multiplication by planting new congregations is a healthy and time-honored method of church growth. It is, in fact, the pattern employed by the early church as recorded in the New Testament. In those days, of course, Christianity was a brand-new movement, and any expansion into new territory involved planting a church, because there was no local body of believers from which to draw. The early Christians, scattered throughout the Roman Empire because of persecution, business interests, or other reasons, carried the gospel with them, and wherever they went new churches sprang up. Some of these believers, like Paul, felt the call of God to take the gospel deliberately into new areas:

> And so I have made it my aim to preach the gospel, not where Christ was named, lest I should build on another man's foundation, but as it is written:
> "To whom He was not announced, they shall see;
> And those who have not heard shall understand."
> —Romans 15:20-21

Considering the changes our culture has undergone over the last twenty to thirty years and the increasing number of immigrants from non-Christian countries that now live in the United States, we are finding more and more people in our neighborhoods and communities who have little or no knowledge of the gospel of Christ. For this reason, planting new churches today may not be as different as we might imagine from Paul's experience of taking the gospel where Christ had not been named.

Understanding the distinction between a satellite or extension church and a church plant is of primary importance. A satellite church is a body of believers that is an extension of the mother church and remains one with it in every essential way except location. For example, the Cathedral International consists of the mother church in Perth Amboy, New Jersey, and two satellite congregations in nearby communities. We are essentially one church in three locations. Preaching, teaching, Christian education, and ministry are done at all three locations, but everything is under the authority and oversight of the mother church in Perth Amboy. The oversight of all three locations is carried out through one central pastoral, business, and financial administration.

A church plant, on the other hand, is a new congregation established in a community with the deliberate intention and goal of becoming an independent, self-sustaining church. In its early stages, the new church is similar to a satellite in that it is supported financially, and in every other way, by the mother or sponsoring church and is under the authority and oversight of that church. Some denominations refer to a church plant at this stage of development as a "mission church." Eventually, when the church plant has grown sufficiently to support itself financially and operate its own ministries, it will incorporate as an independent church. Churches planted by the Cathedral International will at this point become a part of the fellowship of churches I serve as bishop: Covenant Ecumenical Fellowship and Cathedral Assemblies, a body that provides connection and apostolic covering to pastors and churches. ("Apostolic covering" is for those pastors who desire to be relationally connected to a presiding bishop for personal mentoring while retaining their ecclesial authority in their respective denominations.)

In the end the question of whether a church should establish a satellite or plant a church will depend on a number of factors, including the location, target group (whom the church is trying to reach), saturation level (the number of Bible-believing, gospel-preaching churches in the target area and how well they are reaching the target group already), church's vision, pastor's leadership, and most of all, Holy Spirit's leading.

Before we establish a satellite congregation or plant a new church, we must consider several important principles to ensure the greatest probability of success. Following are eight of them:

1. Don't Go Unless You Are Sent. While not going unless you are sent by God may seem obvious, it bears emphasizing here. Nothing we do for the kingdom of God, either individually or corporately, should come about purely of our own will and choice. We need to have the clear call and direction of God. This is just as true of starting a satellite or planting a new church as of anything else. Not every church is called to plant a new church just as not every believer is called to become part of a new church plant. Those who are called should go; those who are not should not. Many churches and individual believers have made the mistake of assuming that to see the need is to feel the call. This is not necessarily so. It is important to recognize the need, but then we need to pray and seek God's direction. Only God can issue the call.

Unfortunately, many new churches are started for the wrong reasons and, as a result, usually struggle just to survive, much less grow. Sometimes disgruntled believers will leave one church to start their own, taking their hurt, anger, and bitterness with them while leaving a gaping, bloody, and painful wound in the church from which they departed. It is not impossible for the Lord to bless a church started under such circumstances, but it almost surely will not happen until the people in the new church unpack the bitter baggage they brought with them. Otherwise, they will be starting off with a wide-open foothold for the enemy, who will waste no time stirring up further division and discontent.

Another bad reason to start a new work is because we saw someone else do it successfully. Jumping on the bandwagon is a favorite sport for many churches, particularly those that have not clearly identified their particular vision and mission. It is never wise to try to duplicate someone else's achievement just because it worked for them. What worked for a church in Denver may not work for a church in Newark. What succeeded for a church in Atlanta may fail big-time for a church in Philadelphia. Just because it worked somewhere else does not necessarily mean that it is God's will for your church.

Don't go where you have not been sent. Wait on the Lord and let him confirm the call. He will show you the way.

2. Wait for the Right Time. Launching a satellite congregation or a new church at the wrong time will greatly increase the likelihood of failure no matter how well prepared everything else is. Timing is critical. Ecclesiastes 3:1 says, "To everything there is a season, a time for every purpose under heaven." This means that there is a right time and a wrong time for everything, including starting a new congregation or church. Sometimes, in our zeal and enthusiasm to do the Lord's work, we jump into something before we are ready. Regrettably, we pay for this lack of preparation by consuming much time, energy, and resources to make up for our haste. At other times we may miss God's initiative. We should try to be discerning in both instances.

How can we know when the timing is right to start a new church? First, there must be a witness in the Spirit. Look for signs. There should be an inner witness of the Holy Spirit and a confirming voice from the Lord. Second, are the people ready? Is the congregation as a whole committed to the adventure and the responsibility of planting a new work? They won't get that way by themselves—at least not usually. Growth through multiplication is a principle that must be preached and taught consistently so that the people can internalize it and own it as a fundamental philosophy of church growth. It must be part of the church's identified vision and mission. One sign that the time is right is when a general consensus exists among the people that a new work is needed.

Third, are the necessary resources of money, material, and people available and in place? In other words, has advance preparation been done in anticipation of starting a new work? Because the Christian life (both individual and corporate) is a life of faith, rarely will we have absolutely everything we think we need at the very beginning. Some things we will have to trust God to provide along the way.

Preparation is crucial. Starting a new church is too big of an undertaking to jump in on impulse and only afterwards consider the cost. Jesus said, "For which of you, intending to build a tower, does not sit down first and count the cost, whether he has enough to finish it—lest, after he has laid the foundation, and is not able to finish it, all who see it begin to mock him, saying, 'This man began to build and was not able to finish'" (Luke 14:28-30). King David wanted to build a temple for God, but the Lord told him the task would fall to his son Solomon. The time wasn't right. David then made all the preparations and plans and secured all the building materials before he died. After Solomon ascended the throne, he spent seven years building the temple for which his father had prepared.

Fourth, and most important, the Lord himself will reveal when the time is right. Whether through prayer, Bible study, circumstances, other people in the church, or a combination of these, the Lord will make the right time known. We simply need to make ourselves sensitive and available to listen for when God says, "Now is the time."

3. Find the Right Location. After timing, the next consideration in church planting is finding the right location. Preliminary investigation of this question can begin even before the timing is confirmed so that when the time is right, the church will be ready to move. It is also reasonable to anticipate that when the Lord confirms the timing he will also reveal or confirm the location. Sometimes it will come as a feeling—a witness deep in the spirit of the pastor or some other sensitive leader or church member.

Waiting for the Lord to reveal both the timing and location is vital to avoid missing a season to plant. The apostle Paul was a missionary and church planter who always looked to the Holy Spirit for direction in focusing his evangelistic efforts.

> Now when they had gone through Phrygia and the region of Galatia, they were forbidden by the Holy Spirit to preach the word in Asia. After they had come to Mysia, they tried to go into Bithynia, but the Spirit did not permit them. So passing by Mysia, they came down to Troas. And a vision appeared to Paul in the night. A man of Macedonia stood and pleaded with him, saying, "Come over to Macedonia and help us." Now after he had seen the vision, immediately we sought to go to Macedonia, concluding that the Lord had called us to preach the gospel to them.
> —Acts 16:6-10

The time was right and so was the location. Paul and his companions proceeded to the city of Philippi, where a woman named Lydia became the first known convert to Christ on the continent of Europe, and her home possibly became the meeting place for the fledgling church Paul established in that city.

Even though we should depend on the Lord to reveal the location, there are some practical things we can look for also to help in making the determination. God works in part through practical consideration. For example, are there any new people coming to the church from the same general area of the community or a nearby community that might be a clue as to where the new church plant or satellite is most needed? Door-to-door neighborhood surveys or even "windshield canvassing"—driving through different neighborhoods to get a visual picture of demographics, local needs, and available land and/or buildings—can be useful in getting a feel for the right location.

Sometimes a church member or family will recognize the need for a church in their own neighborhood. They may even be aware of potential locations for the satellite or church plant. That family could become one of the core families in launching the new work. Their home might even serve as the temporary initial meeting place.

One precaution concerning location: diligent research is vital when looking to buy land or an existing building. Many communities have regulations or restrictions that place limits on where churches can locate. Don't invest in property only to find out later that it can't be used for a church facility.

4. Determine How to Start. Depending on demographics, identified needs, availability of a meeting place, and other factors, any number of things can be the catalyst for a new church. In some cases, the right place to begin may be to establish a "preaching point," a place where a simple service of worship and preaching is held once or twice a week, perhaps in a private home or a rented storefront. As people in the neighborhood are drawn to the services and brought to faith in Christ, they often can become the nucleus of a new congregation. This is very likely the pattern that Paul usually followed.

Other circumstances may indicate that the best place to start is with a weekly small group Bible study held preferably in the home of a family that lives in the target area. A small group study outside the traditional church walls is an intimate and nonthreatening way to draw unchurched people into contact with the Word of God. Another plus to this approach is that small group members often develop deep and lasting relationships with one another, which is a very important element for successfully developing a church. The small group Bible study is a time-tested method of church planting and is the favored approach of many church planting experts and formal church planting study programs.

A third possible approach to starting a satellite or planting a new work is to begin by taking a needed ministry into a target area on a regular basis. An economically depressed neighborhood, for example, might benefit from a program of free or nominal-charge daycare for children of working parents who cannot afford other kinds of formal daycare. This is just one of many possibilities. The significant thing is that addressing a legitimate need in the name of Christ helps establish a beachhead in a neighborhood or community that, over time and with careful nurturing, could grow into a new congregation.

5. Build Strong Relationships between the Mother Church and the New Work.
One critical key to the success of any new work, whether a satellite or a church plant, is to build and maintain strong relationships between the mother or sponsoring church and the new congregation. This happens naturally in the early days of the work when the new church is dependent on the sponsor for everything from financial support to pulpit supply to teaching staff for Sunday school and vacation Bible school.

Once the new work begins to stand on its own two feet, however, it is easy for these relationships to shift and drift slowly apart. In the case of a satellite, this is not as major a concern because it is anatomically part of the parent body in every way except physical location. The danger of a relational drift is greater for a church plant because the intention from the beginning is for it to grow to independent status. Nevertheless, even an independence-minded church plant needs ongoing nurturing relationships with its parent congregation.

One obvious way to foster relationship building is for the preaching pastors of the two congregations to switch places occasionally. Experienced teachers from the parent congregation could mentor and assist teachers from the new church and, on occasion, switch places also. Aside from sharing preaching and teaching staff, there are other practical ways to build strong relationships between the mother church and the new work. Occasional joint meetings where both congregations come together for a conference or a seminar or a series of revival meetings can foster a deep sense of kinship. If space permits and the distance between the groups is not too great, such series of meetings could even rotate locations. In addition, members of the parent congregation could be encouraged to visit the other group on occasion and even volunteer to help with some of their outreach ministries.

Perhaps the most critical relationship of all to ensure success is the relationship between the senior pastor of the parent church and the pastor of the new church. It is incumbent on the pastor of the sponsoring body to initiate a positive relationship of mentoring, encouragement, and respect with his or her counterpart in the new work. If jealousy, animosity, or "bad blood" exists between these two leaders, it won't be long before that infection spreads through both congregations with tragic results. The goal of this most important of relationships should be to reflect the relationships that Paul enjoyed with Timothy and also with Titus, his two young protégés in ministry:

> Paul, an apostle of Jesus Christ . . . to Timothy, a *true son* in the faith. (1 Timothy 1:1-2 emphasis added)

> Paul, an apostle of Jesus Christ . . . to Timothy, a *beloved son.* (2 Timothy 1:1-2, emphasis added)

> Paul, a bondservant of God and an apostle of Jesus Christ . . . to Titus, a *true son* in our common faith. (Titus 1:1-4)

6. Be Willing to Take Risks, but Don't Be Impulsive. Launching a satellite congregation or planting a new church is by nature risky business, and anyone who would be involved in it must be willing to take some risks. All pastors who desire to plant must recognize that church planting requires a deep walk of faith. Planting a church or launching a new congregation involves the expenditure of a lot of time, energy, and money—for something that may not work. From a purely human perspective it may all appear to be a waste. William Carey, a Baptist shoemaker from England, went to India as a missionary in the early 1800s; he labored there for *ten years* before he saw his first convert to Christ. I'm sure that in the eyes of many, Carey seemed to be wasting his life—so much time and energy for so small a return. But God's economy is different from ours. *No investment risked for God is ever wasted.* The returns on our investment may be long in coming; in fact, we may not even see them in this life. But if God is in it, our investment will produce abundant returns in God's own time and God's own way. Our responsibility is to be obedient.

Then there is the risk of rejection. Every time we reach out to people in the name and love of Jesus, we make ourselves vulnerable. Not everyone will understand or receive or appreciate the love and help we offer. They may even reject us outright. Let's be honest: rejection hurts. But let us also remember that we are in good company, because our Lord was rejected also. Speaking prophetically of Jesus, Isaiah said:

> He is despised and rejected by men,
> A Man of sorrows and acquainted with grief.
> And we hid, as it were, *our* faces from Him;
> He was despised, and we did not esteem Him.
> —Isaiah 53:3

Nevertheless, there is good news: for every person who rejects us, there will likely be ten others who do not. Most people respond favorably to genuine expressions of love, kindness, and compassion. Most people are hungry for the hope that is found in Christ;

they simply need to hear the gospel expressed in language they can understand by someone who loves them.

One word of caution: take risks, but don't be impulsive. Visionary leaders tend to be impulsive, sometimes acting without thinking things through—stepping out ahead of the Holy Spirit—which usually leads to mistakes. On the flip side, we must not let fear of making a mistake keep us from acting at all. Taking risks, even in God's service, guarantees that some mistakes will occur along the way; after all, we're only human. But God can forgive our mistakes and by his grace turn them into something that will bring him glory.

7. Don't Be Afraid of Failure. Anyone willing to take risks must also be willing to fail on occasion. Don't be afraid to fail; failure is part of learning. There is nothing wrong with failure (except the failure to try) as long as we are willing to learn from our failures. Someone has said that a successful person is a failure who kept trying, who got back up one time more than he was knocked down.

There is no guarantee that every effort we make at starting a new church will succeed. And a failure does not necessarily mean that our vision was wrong or that we missed God. The timing may have been wrong or the failure may have been due to the actions and choices of people over whom we had no control. In some cases we may never know why it failed. The reason may be hidden by God's own design and purpose.

If we have the right attitude and willingness to learn from the experience, failure can propel us to greater maturity and growth; it can help prepare us for future success. Moreover, failure can help us understand how weak and powerless we are in our own resources and therefore how dependent we are on God. It can teach us to "boast in [our] infirmities," like Paul, so that Christ can be glorified in our weakness: "He said to me, 'My grace is sufficient for you, for My strength is made perfect in weakness.'

Therefore most gladly I will rather boast in my infirmities, that the power of Christ may rest upon me. Therefore I take pleasure in infirmities, in reproaches, in needs, in persecutions, in distresses, for Christ's sake. For when I am weak, then I am strong" (2 Corinthians 12:9-10). Failure on occasion is inevitable, so don't fear it. And above all, don't let failure keep you or your church from trying again. Evaluate what happened, learn from the experience, and press on in the confidence that if you are obeying God, he will lead you to success. He just may have some things for you to learn along the way.

8. Don't Make Leaders Too Soon. My final word on this topic is *don't make leaders too soon.* That is one of the most common mistakes that occurs in the process of starting a new church, whether a satellite or a church plant. In the early stages, human resources (particularly leaders) are often scarce, and it becomes very tempting to fill a leadership slot with anyone who is willing to take it, whether or not the person is qualified. In almost every case it is better in the long run to leave a position empty than to fill it with the wrong person. Otherwise, we set up the unqualified leader for failure and may end up disheartening that person to the point that he or she leaves the ministry or even the church. The whole body will suffer as a consequence.

People seek leadership for many different reasons. Some have control issues, a burning need to be "in charge." Others have a need for approval and acceptance. Some may be angry with their last pastor and hope to hurt him or her by leading a different group. Then there are new Christians who have the best of intentions and a sincere desire to lead yet lack seasoning and spiritual maturity, discernment, and wisdom.

In 1 Timothy 3:3-7 Paul gives Timothy guidelines for selecting bishops for the church. One of these guidelines is that the bishop (or leader) must not be a "novice" (v. 6). The Greek word for "novice" is *neophutos*, from which our English word *neophyte* comes. *Neophutos* literally means "newly planted," and in the figurative sense refers to a new or young convert.

There is no hard-and-fast rule for how long to wait before designating leaders. Each new church and every new situation is different. I once advised a pastor of a new work to wait five years before ordaining or appointing any leaders. Others I have told to wait two years or three. Again it depends on the situation. The important thing is to allow sufficient time to get to know potential leaders' hearts and spirits, gifts and temperament; time to train them and let them get some seasoning and spiritual maturity before putting them in front of the people.

Planting a new church and watching it grow to maturity is one of the most exciting and fulfilling events that can happen in the life of an established church. It is very much akin to the joy of giving birth—not to mention it involves labor pains along the way! Jesus said, "A woman, when she is in labor, has sorrow because her hour has come; but as soon as she has given birth to the child, she no longer remembers the anguish, for joy that a human being has been born into the world" (John 16:21). It is the same for a "mother" church when its "child," a new congregation, comes forth and grows to become a great light in the darkness and a powerful voice for truth in a world filled with error.

Truly, there is no more satisfying means of church growth than to grow through multiplication. And these few principles are vital to the success of beginning new congregations.

Action Steps
1. *Wait for the right time.* The preaching pastor should wait for signs, usually a confirming word from a covering pastor in unison with a personal affirmation from the Holy Spirit. Never start a new church plant out of bitterness or disappointment.

2. *Find the right location.* Exhaustive demographical surveys will give the preaching pastor a sense of the community in which a church is to be planted.

3. *Determine where to start.* The preaching pastor should consider whether the congregation will start in a private home, storefront, or a rented space. One should consider how many services will be developed during the course of the week. Typically there is one teaching service during the week and a preaching service on Sunday. Be sure to consider what starting time best suits the needs of the local community.

4. *Be willing to take risks.* Do not be afraid to think creatively when constructing a worship service. Consider the needs of your specific context. If your city or region needs a Bible school on wheels for youth, develop it! If God has called you to minister to an economically decayed area, respond to the call. Get to know the needs of your community, and meet those needs through the power of Jesus Christ.

5. *Don't be afraid to fail.* Step out on faith. Think outside the box. If you have developed a ministry that bears little fruit, yet you received confirmation from the Lord that your ministry has been called for this season, be patient and wait on the Lord. Nothing sown into the Kingdom-of-God agenda returns void.

6. *Don't make leaders too soon.* Allow time, and the Holy Spirit will show you those who are ready to assume positions of leadership in the church. Learn the hearts of those who labor among you, and you will be better prepared to discern who is best suited for the positions that need to be filled.

7. *After planting your church, pursue the methods that best fortify your vision.* For example, the preaching pastors of two congregations might switch places occasionally. Experienced teachers from the parent congregation could mentor and assist teachers from the new church and, on occasion, switch places also.

11. the church at its best

✖ ✖ ✖ ✖ ✖ ✖

As indicated in previous chapters, church growth is multifaceted and complex. The centrality of Christ, biblical preaching, purposeful prayer, dynamic worship, sound doctrine, comprehensive Christian education, holy living, tithing, and a balanced orientation toward people all contribute to a church's ability to grow.

In defining true and healthy church growth, we must understand the relationship between qualitative increase, defined in terms of spiritual maturity, and quantitative increase, defined by numerical and financial growth. Although these two ways of assessing growth are often interrelated, they are not the same, nor are they interchangeable. Spiritual growth may or may not lead to numerical and financial growth, while numerical and financial growth *by themselves* will never lead to spiritual growth. Increases in numbers and wealth may make a church bigger, but apart from spiritual growth they will never make a church *better*.

Healthy churches grow because of their commitment as baptized believers and followers of Jesus Christ to love, sacrifice, prayer, and worship. Such churches are bound together by a common vision and call to proclaim Christ to a lost world and to minister in his name to the needs of others. Any group of people that does not function in this manner is not acting as a church no matter what they may call themselves. Such social groups should expect to see little or no growth in the biblical sense of the word.

That said, the church at its best is a growing church, a church vibrant with the life of the Spirit of God and fired with the vision of reaching its community—and beyond—with the good news of the saving power of Jesus Christ. Such is the commission of the church and its very reason for existing.

Growth is the most telling sign of life. The key to the life and growth of a church is for every believer to recognize the importance of maintaining an intimate connection with the Lord, who is our source of life. Jesus emphasized the vital nature of this connection when he said:

> "I am the true vine, and My Father is the vinedresser. Every branch in Me that does not bear fruit He takes away; and every branch that bears fruit He prunes, that it may bear more fruit. . . . Abide in Me, and I in you. As the branch cannot bear fruit of itself, unless it abides in the vine, neither can you, unless you abide in Me.
> —John 15:1-2, 4

Just as growth is the evidence of life, the evidence of growth is fruit bearing. It is possible to give the *appearance* of life on the outside yet not produce any fruit. Beware of the grubs. I live in a rural part of New Jersey where the lawns are green and lush. Last summer my lawn began to die out, patch by patch, and I wanted to know why. At first I thought the grass was burnt from overexposure to the sun or overfertilization. Finally, a landscaper, after scraping off random patches throughout the yard, determined that the problem was not the sun or fertilizer, but grubs! Slimy, cream-colored grubs had begun to eat away the root system, leaving massive destruction.

Even the strongest of congregations needs to be most careful in controlling grubs, people intent on sowing seeds of discontent, before they kill off the congregation. Regardless of outward appearances, grubs can be at work undermining the life and integrity of the congregation. Regrettably, by the time we notice the decay, it is sometimes too late, because the roots have been severed. We must remain diligent in spiritual warfare, maintain one vision for the household of faith, and walk in the unity of the Spirit and the bond of peace. Strong, vibrant, growing churches don't just happen; they grow on purpose.

Fruitlessness can also be a sign of death. Recall the story of Jesus cursing the fig tree. Jesus was returning to Jerusalem one morning and was hungry: "And seeing a fig tree by the road, He came to it and found nothing on it but leaves, and said to it, 'Let no fruit grow on you ever again.' Immediately the fig tree withered away" (Matthew 21:19). Jesus merely hastened the process so that the tree showed on the outside what had already happened on the inside.

The Lord takes the fruitfulness (and lack of fruit) of his people very seriously, as indicated in the following parable:

> A certain man had a fig tree planted in his vineyard, and he came seeking fruit on it and found none. Then he said to the keeper of his vineyard, "Look, for three years I have come seeking fruit on this fig tree and find none. Cut it down; why does it use up the ground?" But he answered and said to him, "Sir, let it alone this year also, until I dig around it and fertilize it. And if it bears fruit, well. But if not, after that you can cut it down."
> —Luke 13:6-9

Sustained fruitlessness is deadly for a church just as much as for any other living organism. And the true church *is* a living organism. Jesus said that we can tell true prophets from the false by their fruits: "You will know them by their fruits. Do men gather grapes from thornbushes or figs from thistles? Even so, every good tree bears good fruit, but a bad tree bears bad fruit. A good tree cannot bear bad fruit, nor can a bad tree bear good fruit. Every tree that does not bear good fruit is cut down and thrown into the fire. Therefore by their fruits you will know them" (Matthew 7:16-20).

How will other people know us? Individually or corporately, what kind of fruit are we showing to the world? When we abide in Christ, the Vine, the Holy Spirit is free to produce in us the fruits of righteousness. Paul said, "The fruit of the Spirit is love, joy, peace, longsuffering, kindness, goodness, faithfulness, gentleness, self-control. Against such there is no law" (Galatians 5:22-23). Because these qualities are in truth very rare in the world in their pure form, when people see them on display in the life and ministry of a church, they will be drawn to that church. Of course, not everyone will respond positively, just as not everyone responded positively to the life, love, and compassion of Jesus Christ. There will always be some who reject us and our message. But if we are true to our vision, our call, and our Lord, many will be drawn into the kingdom of God.

Church growth by definition applies to churches that are alive with the life of the Spirit. What are the signs of that life in a church, and how does that life reveal itself to the world? That is really what I have been defining throughout this book. In this closing chapter, let's examine this life more closely as a summary of what we have learned.

The Greatest of These Is Love

The signs that reveal life in a church are also the signs that define a growing church, because the two are one and the same. A living church is a growing church. And the greatest of these signs of life is *love*.

Paul said that without love, anything else we say or do is as meaningless as "sounding brass or a clanging cymbal" (1 Corinthians 13:1). Without love all of our gifts, talents, abilities, and efforts amount to nothing. We can pray great prayers, preach powerful sermons, sing heart-thrilling worship music, offer ministries to address every need, and provide Bible teaching that is theologically and doctrinally correct with every *i* dotted and every *t* crossed. But unless we are motivated by love for the Lord and for the people who need him, it will all mean nothing in the end.

Jesus said to his disciples, "A new commandment I give to you, that you love one another; as I have loved you, that you also love one another. By this all will know that you are My disciples, if you have love for one another" (John 13:34-35). Love shows the world that we are genuine—that we mean what we say, practice what we preach, live what we believe. These verses in fact imply that the love we display in the church toward one another is the *only* real evidence we can give the world that we are genuine. It is one thing to preach and teach about love but another thing to live love every day—and the world will see the difference.

Our love for God and for one another in the church should naturally extend to those outside the church. A lost world knows nothing about genuine love, despite all of its love songs, love poems, and love "experts." The world needs to see true love in action in the lives of God's people. Love is the mission of the church and the very lifeblood of a growing church.

If we want our church to grow, love will be the driving force behind everything we do. We will pray in love, preach in love, worship in love, minister in love, teach in love, and multiply and plant other churches in love. We will *evangelize* in love, *educate* in love, *emancipate* in love, and *empower* in love. Through *love* we will *lift* and *liberate* lost, suffering, and struggling humanity around us.

True love in action and given in the name of Jesus gets people's attention, and once we have their attention, we can tell them about Jesus and the eternal life they can gain through faith in him. Consider this account from the Book of Acts:

> Now Peter and John went up together to the temple at the hour of prayer, the ninth hour. And a certain man lame from his mother's womb was carried, whom they laid daily at the gate of the temple which is called Beautiful, to ask alms from those who entered the temple; who, seeing Peter and John about to go into the temple, asked for alms. And fixing his eyes on him, with John, Peter said, "Look at us." So he gave them his attention, expecting to receive something from them.

Then Peter said, "Silver and gold I do not have, but what I do have I give you: In the name of Jesus Christ of Nazareth, rise up and walk." And he took him by the right hand and lifted him up, and immediately his feet and ankle bones received strength. So he, leaping up, stood and walked and entered the temple with them—walking, leaping, and praising God. And all the people saw him walking and praising God. Then they knew that it was he who sat begging alms at the Beautiful Gate of the temple; and they were filled with wonder and amazement at what had happened to him.

Now as the lame man who was healed held on to Peter and John, all the people ran together to them in the porch which is called Solomon's, greatly amazed. So when Peter saw it, he responded to the people.

—Acts 3:1-12

That day when Peter and John were in the temple, Peter healed the beggar who had been lame from birth. In the love and power of Jesus Christ, Peter enabled the man to walk for the first time in his life. The *love* of Jesus *lifted* this man to his feet and *liberated* him from the bondage of lameness. At the same time it changed his life forever, not just physically, but also spiritually, as he had a firsthand encounter with the God who loved him. This demonstration of divine love and power amazed all the people in the temple precincts who witnessed it, and they quickly surrounded the two apostles and the newly healed man, eager to learn more. This set up an opportunity for Peter to preach the gospel to them.

Love must undergird and permeate all we do, because love is the only thing that will last. We can do many things for other people that will help them in material and physical ways, but all those things will one day pass away. An old song from my youth would remind us regularly, "Remember, only what you do for

Christ will last, only what you do for him will be counted in the end." Only what you do for Christ will last! Paul writes: "Love never fails. But whether there are prophecies, they will fail; whether there are tongues, they will cease; whether there is knowledge, it will vanish away. For we know in part and we prophesy in part. But when that which is perfect has come, then that which is in part will be done away. . . . And now abide faith, hope, love, these three; but the greatest of these is love" (1 Corinthians 13:8-10, 13).

The greatest of these is love. Love fulfills the law. Love promotes church life and health and growth in other ways as well.

One in the Spirit, One in the Lord

One of the things love does in the church is promote unity. When the people of God come together in the unity of mutual love, they make a powerful team. We see this demonstrated in the passage quoted from Acts 3. Peter and John went up to the temple *together*. A growing church—the church at its best—is a church that walks together in unity and works together as a team. Love promotes unity because it seeks out the common things that bind us together and helps us set aside our petty differences. It keeps our focus on *Christ as our center* and assists us in formulating a clear and common vision.

Peter and John went to the *temple* together. A growing church recognizes the importance of everyone in the body being consistently committed to the "temple." Sometimes we are tempted to downplay the importance of regular church attendance. In reality, there is no greater power on earth than a body of local believers gathered together in the unity of common worship, prayer, and proclamation of God's Word. Nothing can substitute for the regular corporate gathering of the saints of God, for something indefinable and wonderful happens in each of us when we enter the holy place where the prayers and praises of the saints go up and the power of the Lord comes down, the place where the walls echo with the Word of God and the atmosphere is permeated with the anointing of the Holy Spirit.

There can be no real power on the church if the church does not press in and pray and praise and walk in unity. Love builds unity, which builds and preserves the church.

Seeing Who Is on the Steps

It was the hour of prayer, and Peter and John were on their way to the temple together to pray. But they were not so intent on their goal that they failed to see the lame beggar on the steps. Sometimes we can get so caught up in our own affairs and agendas that we fail to notice the people around us who need our help. It is easy to try to substitute enthusiastic praise and worship and eloquent preaching and doctrinally correct teaching for compassionate ministry, because compassionate ministry is hands-on, often dirty, and sometimes unpleasant. But there *is* no substitute. Our entire worship, plans, and programs mean nothing if they do not propel us in love onto the steps and into the streets and neighborhoods to lift the lame and fallen and to liberate the beggars and addicts. James asks: "What does it profit, my brethren, if someone says he has faith but does not have works? Can faith save him? If a brother or sister is naked and destitute of daily food, and one of you says to them, 'Depart in peace, be warmed and filled,' but you do not give them the things which are needed for the body, what does it profit? Thus also faith by itself, if it does not have works, is dead" (2:14-17).

A growing church—the church at its best—keeps a constant watch to see who is on its steps, and it immediately takes steps to meet their needs. All we have to do is take a look and we will see the lame, the blind, the abused, the sick, the poverty-stricken, the despairing, the illiterate, the hungry, the naked, the hopeless, the homeless, the addicted, the AIDS-afflicted, the unwed mothers, the outcast, the "mentally lame," the morally confused, the spiritually ignorant, and the lost—all on our steps.

Some churches are overwhelmed by what they see, and they respond by deciding not to look at their steps anymore. It's too painful, too discouraging, too convicting. A growing church, however—a church at its best—will not turn away, but will embrace those who have come to its steps. Lifting the "lame"—no matter what form of lameness we find—will take us out of our comfort zones and into the field of battle. Love does not do what is comfortable; love does what is *right*. It will cost us time, money, energy, blood, sweat, tears (many of them!), heartache, and more than a little pain. But what else can we do? Loving, lifting, and liberating the lost, hurting, and needy people around us is why we are on this earth. It is why Jesus Christ established his church—his body on earth—in the first place and why he called each of us to be part of that body. If as a church we are not loving, lifting, and liberating, then we have abrogated our very reason for existence. We are like the fig tree that Jesus cursed because of its fruitlessness; we may show outward signs of life, but inside we are sick and dying and purposeless, "having a form of godliness but denying its power" (2 Timothy 3:5).

Many churches desiring to grow resort to methods, formulas, plans, and programs, and then they cannot understand why nothing seems to work. They fail to understand that because of their self-centered approach to growth—"What can *we* do to get *our* church to grow?"—they have forgotten that the work and ministry of the church is and must be *outward-focused*—not growth for its own sake or just to fill the pews or increase the bank account, but growth to increase the Kingdom of God.

A growing church—the church at its best—remembers that to be outward-focused means to live daily by the Great Commandment, to love the Lord our God with all our heart, soul, mind, and strength and to love our neighbors as ourselves; and by the Great Commission, to go and make disciples of all nations, baptizing them in the name of the Father, the Son, and the Holy Spirit, teaching them to observe everything Jesus taught.

Helping People Who Are Disabled Walk Again

A growing church—the church at its best—knows that it is in the business of helping the lame walk again. There are many different ways to be "disabled": physically, mentally, emotionally, spiritually. All of us as believers were formerly disabled in one way or another. And we all are still in the process of being healed. Our healing will not be complete and perfected until we get to heaven. So, if we all have disabilities, then we who have been healed by Jesus are well equipped to witness to those who are still in bondage to their lameness.

Peter and John saw the lame beggar on the temple steps. They called to him, and he focused his attention on them, expecting to receive alms. Instead, Peter said, "Silver and gold I do not have, but what I do have I give you: In the name of Jesus Christ of Nazareth, rise up and walk." Then Peter took him by the hand and lifted him up. The man's ankles were strengthened, and he began walking and leaping for joy. He then entered the temple with Peter and John, walking on his own two feet for the first time in his life.

No government program could help the lame beggar. No welfare plan put strength in his ankles or dignity in his spirit. Only the power of the name of Jesus made him whole and lifted him from his beggar's rags into the fullness of the man he was created to be. Society had written him off as someone to be pitied and the object of self-righteous charity. The power of the name of Jesus changed him. It lifted him up and liberated him forever. Some churches make use of government funds in programs to help the needy. I do not oppose such programs, so long as they are centered in Christ. Again, we must remember the true source of our power.

Because the church is the body of Christ on earth, we have the authority to speak and teach and act in the powerful name of Jesus. A growing church—the church at its best—recognizes that authority and uses it in love, compassion, and humility, always remembering that Christ is the head of his church. We are Jesus' ambassadors to whom he has committed the ministry of reconciliation.

So there really is no real mystery about church growth. Jesus said, "I, if I am lifted up from the earth, will draw all peoples to Myself" (John 12:32). That was his mission on earth, and that is the mission he has given to us, the church: to lift up the name and the person of Jesus Christ in all his power and glory and life-changing authority. As long as we apply ourselves faithfully and diligently to our mission and our commission, our churches will grow and the Kingdom of God will increase. That is God's plan and promise, as spelled out by Jesus in a discussion with his disciples:

> He said to them, "But who do you say that I am?" Simon Peter answered and said, "You are the Christ, the Son of the living God." Jesus answered and said to him: "Blessed are you, Simon Bar-Jonah, for flesh and blood has not revealed this to you, but My Father who is in heaven. And I also say to you that you are Peter, and *on this rock I will build My church, and the gates of Hades shall not prevail against it.*"
> —Matthew 16:15-18 (emphasis added)

Remember that African American churches grow in different ways. Thus, I encourage every pastor and church leader to stay with the vision, the mandate, God gave you. Keep the name of Jesus lifted before you. Pursue a diligent prayer life. Love the people; liberate the poor. God will meet you where you are and transform your life and church with power you never imagined.

notes

☒ ☒ ☒ ☒ ☒ ☒

Chapter 1

1. Gardner C. Taylor, "Our National Treasure," *Gospel Today*, September/October 2005, p. 42.

Chapter 8

1. Paul Laurence Dunbar, "Life," *Lyrics of Lowly Life*, 1896, http://poetry.poetryx.com/poems/6224/, accessed February 13, 2006.